Contemporary Architect's Concept Series 26

Toshiharu Naka | Two Cycles

LIXIL Publishing

Credits

Photo	Koichi Torimura / pp. 8-9, 10-11, 16-17, 18-19, 20-21, 23, 24-25, 38 (top, bottom), 40, 42-43, 49 (top, middle, bottom), 70-71, 74, 76, 80 (right), 82, 98-99, 101, 102, 124-125, 130 (top, bottom), 131, 134 (top, bottom), 135, 139, 149, 152
	Makoto Yoshida / pp. 44 (bottom), 88, 90, 91
	Masao Nishikawa / pp. 86-87, 96-97, 117
	Shinkenchiku-sha / pp. 81, 155
	HITOTOWA INC. / pp. 52-53
	Shotaro Uehara / p. 41
	Naka Architects' Studio / Other than those above

Other	p. 26	Changes in number of employees of clothes-mending businesses and number of sewing-machine shipments. Graph prepared by the author based on figures from the Economic Census of the Statistics Bureau, Ministry of Internal Affairs and Communications, and the Machinery Statistics Yearbook, Ministry of Economy, Trade and Industry
	p. 64	51C-N apartment prototype (draft floor plan by Yoshitake Laboratory). From Shigebumi Suzuki, *White Paper on the 51C: My Postwar History of Architectural Planning* (SUMAI Library Publishing Company, 2006) p. 169.
	p. 66	Kasai Clean Town Seishin Kita Heights, Buildings 4~9. From Hiroshi Moriyasu et al., *Architectural Planning and Design Series 4: Highrise and Super-Highrise Apartment Housing* (Ichigaya Publishing, 1993) p. 108.
	p. 67	Square Tamagawa-Josui. From Architectural Institute of Japan, *Compact Architectural Statistics (Residences), Second Edition* (Maruzen Publishing, 2006) p. 137.
	p. 115	Dependency on others during an individual's lifetime. From Toshio Otsuki, *Home, Town, and Community* (Okokusha, 2017) p. 7.
	p. 120	Supercomputer simulation (partial image). From National Institute for Land and Infrastructure Management, "Images of Ventilation Paths by District" (http://www.nilim.go.jp/lab/bcg/siryou/tnn/tnn0730pdf/ks073010.pdf)
	p. 148	Threshold diagram (text revised by permission of the author). From Riken Yamamoto, *The Space of Power and the Power of Space: Designing Between Personal and State Spaces* (Kodansha, 2015) p. 25.

仲俊治 | 2つの循環

LIXIL出版

目次

1　小さな経済 —— Social な循環

- 1-1　職住混合の住宅 ——《写真家のスタジオ付き住宅》……… 8
- 1-2　Social な循環としての〈小さな経済〉……… 26
- 1-3　中間領域への気づき ——《食堂付きアパート》……… 32
- 1-4　内発的な営みの場 ——《小商いの実験室》……… 50
- 1-5　顔の見える、外部との交流空間としての中間領域
　　　—— Social な循環の可視化 ……… 60

2　自然とともに居ること —— Ecological な循環

- 2-1　屋根付き外部・地続きの床 ——《白馬の山荘》……… 70
- 2-2　建築の群れとしての風景 ——《上総喜望の郷おむかいさん》……… 84
- 2-3　流れのなかに場をつくる ——《深沢の住宅》……… 98
- 2-4　温熱環境的な中間領域 —— Ecological な循環の可視化 ……… 106

3　2つの循環・融合の意図

- 3-1　ヴェネチア・ビエンナーレでの違和感 ……… 110
- 3-2　従来のコミュニティ論への違和感 ……… 114
- 3-3　融合の可能性を感じたきっかけ ……… 118

4　建築を2つの循環のなかに位置づける

- 4-1　2つの循環を重ねる ——《五本木の集合住宅》……… 124
- 4-2　動的なプログラム論 —— 閾論のアップデート ……… 148

Contents

1 Small Economies — A Social Cycle

1-1 A Live/Work House: Photographer's House with Studio ⋯⋯⋯⋯ 8

1-2 Small Economies as a Social Cycle ⋯⋯⋯⋯ 26

1-3 Focusing on Intermediate Areas: Apartments with a Small Restaurant ⋯⋯⋯⋯ 32

1-4 A Place for Spontaneous Activity: Small Business Laboratory ⋯⋯⋯⋯ 50

1-5 The Intermediate Area as a Space for Face-to-Face Interaction with the Outside: Giving Visibility to a Social Cycle ⋯⋯⋯⋯ 60

2 Coexisting with Nature — An Ecological Cycle

2-1 A Roofed Outdoor Space with a Ground-Level Floor: Villa in Hakuba ⋯⋯⋯⋯ 70

2-2 A Landscape of Grouped Houses: Omukai-san ⋯⋯⋯⋯ 84

2-3 Creating Places in a Flow: House in Fukasawa ⋯⋯⋯⋯ 98

2-4 Intermediate Areas as Thermal Environments: Making the Ecological Cycle Visible ⋯⋯⋯⋯ 106

3 The Fusion of the Two Cycles

3-1 Misgivings at the Venice Biennale ⋯⋯⋯⋯ 110

3-2 Misgivings about Conventional Ideas of Community ⋯⋯⋯⋯ 114

3-3 Realizing Possibilities for Fusion ⋯⋯⋯⋯ 118

4 Positioning Architecture within Two Cycles

4-1 Overlaying Two Cycles: Gohongi Housing ⋯⋯⋯⋯ 124

4-2 Dynamic Program Theory: A Threshold Theory Update ⋯⋯⋯⋯ 148

I 小さな経済——Socialな循環

Small Economies—A Social Cycle

1-1 職住混合の住宅──《写真家のスタジオ付き住宅》
A Live/Work House: Photographer's House with Studio

軽井沢近郊の森の中に、写真家のスタジオやオフィスが併設された住宅を設計しました。創作活動と日々の暮らしは分けられるものではなく結びついている、しかし、創作活動のための緊張感は必要である。そんな写真家の考えに共感しました。この建築は樹木の分布を強く意識した構成を持っています。樹木は、時間や季節の移ろいを映し出します。創作活動の気づきを与える存在として、周辺に広がる樹木を活かそうと考えました。

　木々のあいだを狙って、3枚の壁を放射状に立てました。これらの壁は柱・梁・土台に合板を片面から打ち付けただけの、簡素な耐震壁です。これら3枚の耐震壁を背骨とみなして両側に空間を膨らませていき、樹木のあいだに滑り込ませたようなシルエットの建築としました★1。このように建てることで、森の木々を切らないようにもできます。

I designed a residence in the woods of Karuizawa that includes a studio and office for a photographer. I understood the photographer's desire for a place that would integrate rather than separate her creative activities and her daily life, yet still provide the sense of tension needed for creative work. The house therefore has a layout closely attuned to the distribution of the trees around it. Trees reflect the passage of time and the changes of the seasons, so I wanted the woods surrounding the house to be a presence conducive to creative activity.

To accommodate the spaces between the trees, I built three walls in a radial pattern. These were simple earthquake-resistant walls made by affixing plywood on only one side of the columns, beams and sills. Filling out the spaces on both sides of these three spine-like walls, I came up with a structure that appears to be slipped in among the trees. ★1 This design allowed us to proceed without cutting down any of the woods.

★1
背骨のような耐震壁からオフセットした外周壁は、群生する木々の背景として位置づけ、浸透性の高い服飾用の染料で黒色に塗装しました。
I placed the outer walls at an offset from the quake-resistant spine according to how the surrounding trees were grouped, and painted the walls black with a high-permeability decorative stain.

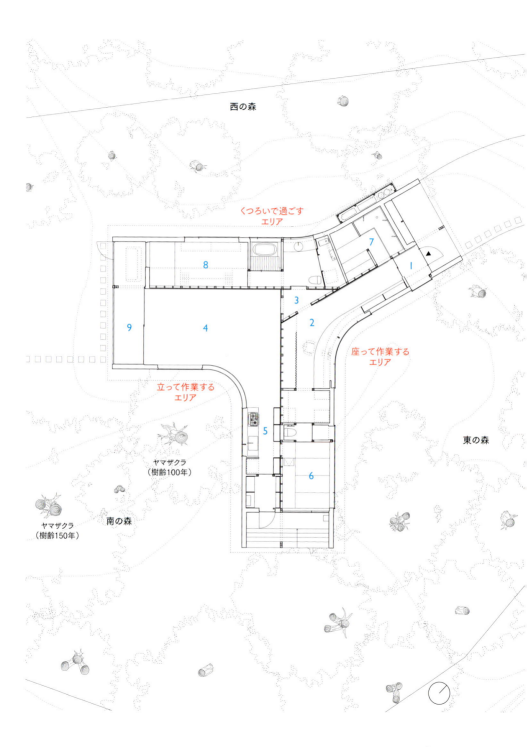

木の勢力範囲
Spheres of influence of trees

木と木のあいだには日が差し込む明るい日溜まりがある
Bright sunny areas between the trees

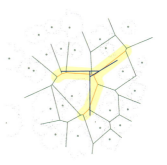

日溜まりに3枚の背骨壁を立てる
Extending three spine-like walls through the sunny areas

平面図 1:200
Plan 1:200

1．エントランス　Entrance
2．オフィス　Office
3．天窓室　Skylight room
4．スタジオ　Studio
5．キッチン　Kitchen
6．和室　*Tatami* room
7．暗室　Darkroom
8．プライベートルーム　Private room
9．蚊帳テラス　Terrace

木に当たらないように注意しながら
厚みを与えて空間化する
Expanding spaces around the walls
without impacting the trees

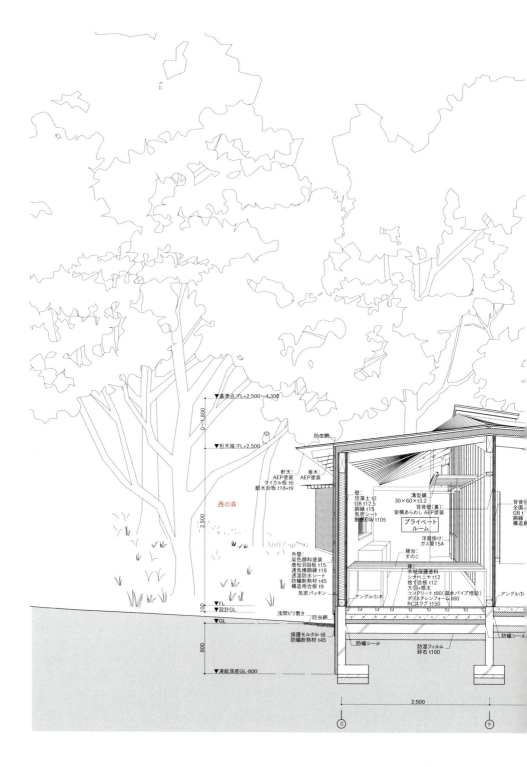

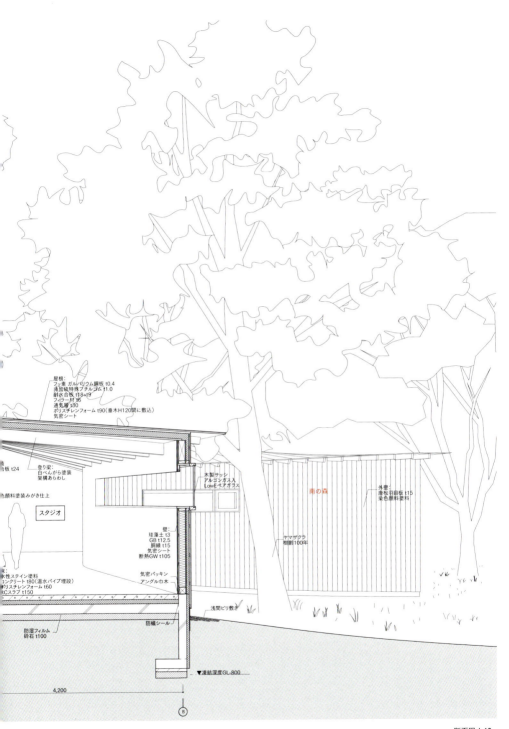

断面図 1:60
Cross Section 1:60

15 | Small Economies—A Social Cycle

なぜ壁は3枚か。

2つの理由があります。ひとつには、敷地一帯はさまざまな樹種が混ざっているように見えますが、観察しているうちに、3種類の樹木がなんとなくまとまって生えていることが見えてきました。2本の桜の老樹(樹齢100年以上!)、大きなカエデたち、そしてクリの木です。敷地はこれらの勢力範囲の狭間という特異点に思え、樹種の違いを建築内部から楽しめる建築にしようと思ったのです。

もうひとつの理由が、冒頭の話になりますが、住む空間／働く空間という分け方でない組織の仕方を考えたかったからです。職住一体の建築として、どのような組織の仕方があるのか。結果的に、所作に応じて空間を組織することにしました。立って作業する、座って作業する、くつろいでいる、という3種類です。立位ゾーンは、作業場としてのスタジオのほかに、キッチンもあります。開口部は高めの位置に設け、桜の大木をすこし上に眺める空間としています。座位ゾーンにはオフィススペースや和室が配置されます。座ったときに、カエデの垂れた枝先が印象的に見えることを考慮して開口部をデザインしています。クリの木が群生している北側には寝室や水まわりといった空間を配置し、くつろぎつつ内省するような空間としました。北側の地面は緩やかに上がっていくために、限定的に設けた開口からは、地面を柔らかく覆う下草が印象的に見えます。

Why three walls?

I had two reasons. First, although the lot at first glance appeared to have a mix of many different kinds of tree, closer observation showed that most of the growth consisted of three species: two very old cherries (over a century old!), several large maples, and some chestnuts. Thinking of the lot as a singularity where the spheres of influence of these species intersected, I decided to build a house that would allow its inhabitants to enjoy the diversity of species outside.

My second reason was the client's aforementioned desire for a layout that did not differentiate between living and working spaces. What sort of arrangement was appropriate for a live/work structure? I finally decided to organize the space according to the client's activities, of which there were three types: working while standing, working while sitting, and relaxing. The standing zone contains not only the studio but also the kitchen. Apertures are located high on the wall so that one can gaze slightly upward at the big cherry trees. The sitting zone has office space as well as a Japanese-style room. Here I designed the apertures so that one can enjoy, while sitting, a lyrical view of the spreading maple branches. I placed the bedroom and wet area on the north side where the chestnut trees grew in a cluster, enhancing a space for relaxation and contemplation. Because the land gently rises here, the limited apertures in this section afford a soothing view of the soft carpet of vegetation covering the ground.

壁を放射状に配置したことに加え、中心に向かって空間を高くすることにより、内部を動き回る際の空間体験に抑揚を与えようと考えました。各ゾーンの端部に行くほど天井は低くなり、屋外に押し出されるような感覚を得ます★2。反対に、中心に向かうほど大きく包まれるような安定感があります。中心に向かうとき、中心から離れるとき、そのそれぞれで空間体験が異なることになります。さらに、この建築の中心で3枚の壁は交差するのですが、この部分を通らないと壁の反対側には行けません★3。中心部分の全面トップライトは、この体験をより印象的なものにします★4。

★2
各ゾーンの端部は、屋根付きの屋外の居場所となっています。脱着可能な蚊帳によって、虫の入らない半屋外空間としました。このディテール検討には気合を入れて臨みましたが、うまくいったと思います。

The outer edge of each zone functions as a roofed outdoor living area. Detachable mosquito netting turns these spaces into insect-proof semi-outdoor spaces. I invested considerable effort in developing this detail, with what I think are favorable results.

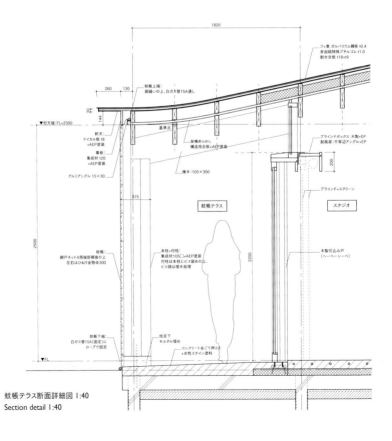

蚊帳テラス断面詳細図 1:40
Section detail 1:40

In addition to laying the walls out radially, I made the interior space higher toward the center so as to modulate the spatial experience of moving around inside the house. As one approaches the far end of each zone the ceiling gets lower, imparting a sensation of being pushed toward the exterior.★2 Conversely, approaching the center gives one a feeling of envelopment and security. Thus the spatial experience varies depending on whether one is moving toward or away from the center. Furthermore, where the three walls intersect at the center of the structure they enclose a space that one must pass through to cross over to the opposite side.★3 I covered this central space with a skylight to accentuate the experience of moving through it.★4

★3
交差のさせ方は建築デザイン上のポイントになっています。3枚の耐震壁をズレながら交差させることで、構造的に安定した中心を持つ建築としています。ズレながら交差するために空間が生まれるわけですが、この空間によって、3つのゾーンが独立的に感じられることを意図してもいます。

How to effect this intersection was a critical aspect of the structure's design. Staggering the meeting points of the three quake-resistant walls gives the building a structurally stable center. The space created by this staggered layout also enhances the sense of autonomy among the three zones.

★4
周囲の三方を山に囲まれた谷底の土地にあり、建築の中心を光で満たしたいと考えました。トップライトは拡散光になるようにフロストガラスを用い、さらにトップライト下に細かいルーバーを配置しています。このルーバーは、トップライトの枠部材を隠すためであり、抽象化された光だけがある、という状態にしようとしました。

Because the lot is on the floor of a valley with mountains on three sides, I wanted to fill the center of the house with light. To diffuse incoming light I used frosted glass for the skylight and placed thin louvers under it, which also serve to conceal the frame. My aim was to make the incoming light "abstract."

森の中という社会的文脈がない場所において、住む空間／働く空間の融合のあり方を純粋培養した格好です。身体の所作と周辺環境との関係のなかで、融合のあり方を求めようとしました。動くたびに発見があるような建築として。このプロジェクトを通して、職住の融合ということが建築デザインの課題になりえると確信しました。

Achieving a fusion of living and working spaces in a house in the woods, without the usual social context, was a bit like working up a pure culture in a lab. I sought clues for this fusion in the physical movements of the client and their relationship to the surrounding environment; I wanted each movement to yield new discoveries. This project gave me the certainty that live/work integration can be a significant theme of architectural design.

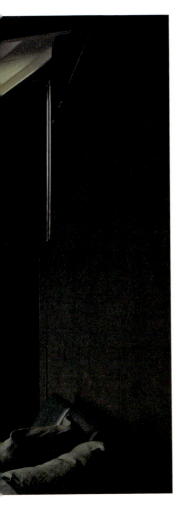

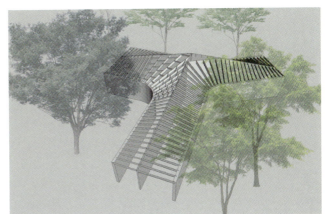

I–2　Socialな循環としての〈小さな経済〉

Small Economies as a Social Cycle

　生業のあり方は住宅、ひいては都市のデザインにとって決定的に重要だ——個人の仕事場やお店が併設された住宅を設計したり、興味深い事例を集めたりしていくうちに、そう考えるようになりました。そして、生業のあり方そのものが変わりつつあるという予感も。住宅を改造してその一部につくられたチーズケーキ屋さんは、改修によって現れたファサードがユニークだし、その前の道路がいつも掃き清められています。

　僕の自宅から駅に行く途中には小さなかけはぎ屋さんがあり、その仕事場は玄関脇にあります★5。

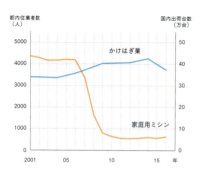

かけはぎ業従業者数、ミシン出荷台数の変遷
Changes in number of employees of clothes-mending businesses and number of sewing-machine shipments.

People's livelihoods are a critical factor in the design of residences, and indeed of entire cities. This is something I began to realize in the course of seeing many examples, including some I designed, of residences combined with the owner's workplace or shop. It further struck me that a change is taking place in how we work. When a client remodeled his house and turned part of it into a cheesecake shop, the result was a unique new façade, and he always keeps the street in front of it swept clean.

On the way from my home to the nearest train station is a small clothes-mending shop right next to the entrance to the owner's house. ★5

★5
かけはぎ屋さんはどの商店街にも一軒はあるようなお店で〈小さな経済〉の典型例です。かけはぎ屋さんの数と家庭用ミシンの出荷台数の変遷を比べるとおもしろいことがわかります。2001年からの15年間で、家庭用ミシンの出荷台数は40万台から5万台に激減している一方で、東京都におけるかけはぎ業の従業者は約3,400人から約3,700人と、むしろ1割ほど増えています。従来、家庭内で行われていた裁縫が外部化していることを示す、数値的な裏付けと見ることができそうです。

Clothes-mending shops are a classic example of small economies; every shopping street in Japan seems to have at least one. It is interesting to compare the number of such businesses with shipments of home-use sewing machines. In 15 years starting in 2001, machine shipments fell from 400 thousand to 50 thousand units nationwide, but the number of people working as clothes-menders in Tokyo rose 10%, from 3,400 to 3,700. These figures suggest that more and more households are outsourcing sewing work that was once done at home.

小さなお店には不釣り合いなほど大きなガラス面越しに、背筋をピンと伸ばしてミシンをあてる姿が見え、前の通りに緊張感と安心感を与えています。お店や仕事場が住宅に併設されることで芽生える外向きの意識。その意識が建築の表層や街路に現れている事例ばかりです★6。

　顔の見える個人の仕事や、趣味や特技が高じての小商い★7によって金銭を得る営みのことを、〈小さな経済〉と呼ぶことにします★8。ここには、在宅勤務や副業・兼業的なテレワークなどのあたらしい働き方★9も含んでよいでしょう。金額は小さくても構いません。やりがいがそれを補います★10。〈小さな経済〉活動は生業であることもあればそうでないこともありますが、内発的で継続的な活動です。その人が住む場所や地域社会に責任を持ち、地域内での交換が生まれるという重要な特徴があります。〈小さな経済〉は、社会的な関係の循環を促す活動です。すこし広い視野に立てば、情報技術の進展が〈小さな経済〉を可能にし、さらに、そこでは生産と消費の融合という性質の経済活動も見受けられます。

　〈小さな経済〉の特徴を表としてまとめると、次のようになります。

★6
生業に関心を持つことになったきっかけは、建築家・山本理顕さんが提唱する「地域社会圏」という概念の研究会における「地域内ワーク」という考え方についての議論に参加したことでした。地域社会圏は、家庭規模の縮小から、一住宅＝一家族という近代の統治システム・空間モデルを転換し、家庭機能を地域内共同体で補い合うという考え方です。上述のかけはぎ屋さん、つまり裁縫の外部化も実社会における例といえます。
(山本理顕ほか『地域社会圏主義 増補改訂版』LIXIL出版、2013、pp.64-67)
My interest in livelihoods grew out of my participation in discussions of the idea of "local work" in a study group on the concept of "local community areas" posited by the architect Riken Yamamoto. A local community area is defined as a community that supports household functions to compensate for the reduced size of households in an inversion of the modern ruling order and spatial model of "one house = one family." The aforementioned clothes-mending business—i.e., the outsourcing of sewing work—is one real-life example of this trend. See Riken Yamamoto et al., *Chiiki shakai-ken shugi (zoho kaitei-ban)* (Local Community Area Principles, revised and expanded edition), LIXIL Publishing, 2013, pp. 64-67.

★7
URの定義では、「個人や民間団体が自発的に参画できる小規模な商業」。(https://www.ur-net.go.jp/press/h28/ur2016press_0716_misato.pdf)
Defined by the semi-public housing corporation Urban Renaissance (UR) as "small-scale businesses in which individuals or private groups participate at their own initiative" (https://www.ur-net.go.jp/press/h28/ur2016press_0716_misato.pdf).

★8
昨今では、小商い、一坪ビジネスなど、いろいろな表現を目にします。そのような活動のための場づくり――たとえばシェアキッチンのようなものですが――も目にするようになりました。これらの現象は〈小さな経済〉という活動の広がりを映しているように思います。
We recently see a number of terms coming into use for small "one-room" businesses of this sort, as well as the appearance of new structures designed to support such activities. Phenomena like the shared-use kitchen reflect the spread of "small economy" activities, I believe.

The somewhat over-large glass window affords a clear view of the owner hunched over his sewing machine, exuding a mix of tension and tranquility that spills into the street outside. Combining home and workplace engenders an outward-facing sensibility that, in every instance I have seen, makes itself felt in the building's façade and in the street.★6

I refer to small money-earning businesses★7 that consist of the work of a visible individual, or have evolved from a personal hobby or skill, as "small economies."★8 We can include in this category newer forms of at-home work—side businesses, telecommuting and the like.★9 The amount of income is unimportant; meager profits are compensated for by the motivation of the owner.★10 A small economy may or may not be someone's main form of livelihood, but it is always a spontaneously conceived and continuing activity. Such businesses are noteworthy for the responsibility the proprietors demonstrate toward their homes and communities; they are important contributors to community interaction. Small economies promote the circulation of social relations. In a very broad sense, small economies have been made possible by advances in information technology, and they can also be identified as an economic activity characterized by the merger of production and consumption.

The chart below lists the characteristics of small economies.

★9
『日本経済新聞』2018年4月4日の記事によれば、2018年はフリーランスの推定経済規模（推定報酬額）が初めて20兆円を超え、日本の総給与支払額の10%を占める規模に成長しています。ここには従来的な個人事業主も含まれますが、メインの仕事を抱えながら別の仕事をする「副業」と2社以上の企業から雇用される「複業」を合わせると全体の2/3を占めるそうです。また、あたらしい働き方として、ネットで仕事を受注する「クラウドワーカー」は330万人に及ぶとの報道もあります。子育ての隙間時間を活用するなど、在宅勤務との親和性も高いことが窺えます（同紙、2016年11月15日記事）。

According to an article in the April 4, 2018 issue of *Nihon Keizai Shinbun* (Japan Economic News), the estimated economic scale (i.e., estimated income) of freelance work topped 20 trillion yen for the first time in 2018, and now makes up 10% of total remuneration in Japan. Though these figures include traditional sole proprietors, two-thirds of the total consists of people engaged in a sideline in addition to their main job, and people employed at two or more companies.

An article in the November 15, 2016 issue of the same newspaper reported that there are now 3.33 million "cloud workers" in Japan who receive their work via the Internet, and suggested that many find this lifestyle compatible with telecommuting or child-rearing.

★10
金銭に代わるものとして「義理」を挙げる者もいます。「義理を（…）社会の一種のルールであり、しかも金銭の賃借のように、すべての行為を量的に還元して考えることができる便利な性質を持つものであるとするならば（…）」（『都市住宅』1972年10月号「特集＝義理の共同体」上田篤責任編集、鹿島出版会）

Some have suggested that *giri* (social obligation) can function as a substitute for monetary compensation. "We may posit that obligation is one of the rules of society, and that it has the convenient attribute of assigning a quantitative value to all activities, just like a cash loan . . ." ("Special Feature: Communities of Obligation", Atsushi Ueda, ed., *Toshi jutaku* [Urban Housing], October 1972 issue, Kajima Institute Publishing Co., Ltd.)

特徴	具体的現れ
あたらしい働き方	SOHO、一人二役、ちょっとした小遣い稼ぎ
趣味や特技が高じて	楽しさを伴うやりとり、あたらしい相互扶助
情報技術の進展がサポート	スキルをシェアして向上、小口を集めて束にする
大もうけはない場合も自己実現の満足感	GDPにはあまり関係ない(かも)、笑顔
他者や外部を前提とする	開かれている、お店の前はいつもきれい、情報発信
消費×生産の融合	住宅×○○(用途複合)、生業(なりわい)の場としての住宅

　〈小さな経済〉に着目することはしかし、単なる企画の目新しさに留まるわけではありません。仕事場やお店が付属する住宅はどのような「現れ」を持つのか。そもそも、仕事場やお店は住宅のどの部分に設けられるのか。単純な付け足しに留まるのか。あるいはあたらしい住宅像として有機的に融合した姿を見せるのか。建築デザイン論としていえば、〈小さな経済〉はプログラムによって建築を開かせ、都市空間に関係づける手段であり、諸室の配列と境界要素のデザインに関係するといえそうです。

Characteristic	Manifestations
New way of working	SOHO; dual work/home role; extra pocket money
Evolved from hobby or skill	Enjoyable interactions; new modes of mutual support
Supported by IT advances	Improving skills through sharing; pooling investments
Satisfaction even without high profits	Little effect on GDP(?); prioritizing friendly relations
Interaction with others, community	Open, welcoming; clean shopfronts; information exchange
Fusion of consumption+production	Residence+?? (mixed-use), home as place of livelihood

However, we should not focus exclusively on the novelty of projects that incorporate these small economies. How should a residence attached to a workplace or shop "appear"? First of all, to what part of the residence do we attach the workplace or shop? Do we simply add it on, or do we merge them in an organic form—a new style of residence? In terms of architectural design, we could say that the program of a small economy is a means of opening up a structure and connecting it to urban space, and hence involves the layout of rooms and the design of their boundary elements.

1-3 中間領域への気づき——《食堂付きアパート》
Focusing on Intermediate Areas: Apartments with a Small Restaurant

　2014年に《食堂付きアパート》という集合住宅をつくりました。商店街に近い職住がほどよく混ざった下町に建つ、〈小さな経済〉に着目してつくったアパートです。5つのSOHO住宅（仕事場を併設した住宅）、シェアオフィス、そして独立志望のシェフが切り盛りする小さな食堂からなる複合的な建築です。〈小さな経済〉の場を住宅に取り込むと、どのような建築が発想でき、また、都市はどのように描けるのか、ということに取り組みました★11。

　ここで得られた建築的気づきは、中間領域の可能性というものでした。用途が複合することによって、用途間のさまざまな境界面ができます。その境界面はデザインしがいのある、じつに興味深い存在に感じられました。

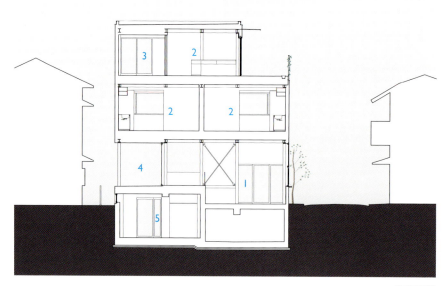

断面図 1:200
Section 1:200

1. 食堂　Restaurant
2. スタジオ　Studio
3. 寝室　Bedroom
4. 路地　Alley
5. シェアオフィス　Shared office

In 2014 I designed an apartment house with a restaurant attached. The structure, which was built with "small economies" in mind, stood in an urban neighborhood with a mix of workplaces and residences, close by a commercial district. It was to contain five residence/SOHO (small office/home office) units, a shared office, and a small restaurant to be managed by a chef with aspirations to go independent. I was interested in what kind of architecture would emerge from incorporating small economies of this sort into a residential building, and how it would affect the cityscape around it. ★11

One architectural revelation I gained from this project was the potential of intermediate areas. In mixed-use structures, various interfaces can be set up between different uses. I realized that these interfaces were truly fascinating spaces from a design standpoint.

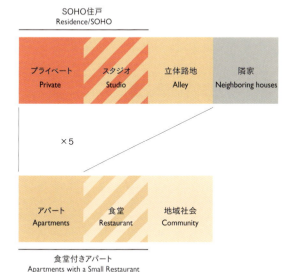

スタジオや食堂を、隣接する空間の中間領域と捉えた
The studios and the restaurant are designed
to serve as intermediate areas between adjoining spaces.

★11
完成してから振り返ると、あたかもこのような複合体がもともと与件としてあったように思われるかもしれません。しかしながら実際は、生業とともにある集合住宅を目指して、クライアントと一緒にもがいていたらこうなった、というのが正しい表現です。

With the benefit of hindsight, one might assume that the resulting composite structure was a given from the start. But in fact, it emerged in this form after many struggles by myself and the client, who wanted to combine an apartment house with places of work.

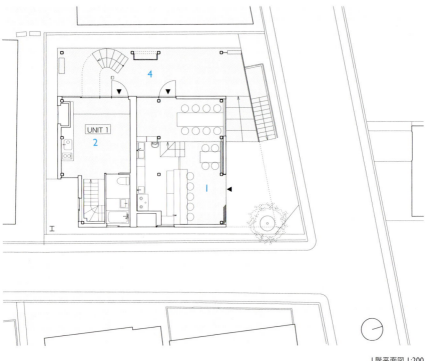

1階平面図 1:200
1F Plan 1:200

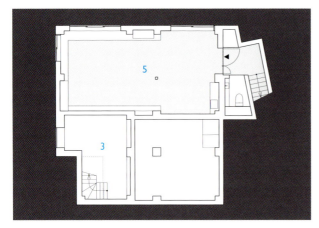

1. 食堂　Restaurant
2. スタジオ　Studio
3. 寝室　Bedroom
4. 路地　Alley
5. シェアオフィス　Shared office

B1階
B1F

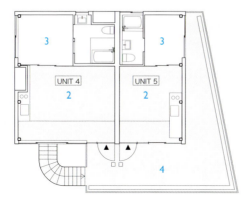

3階
3F

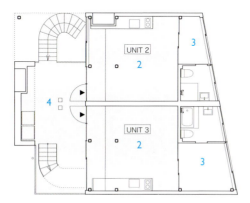

2階
2F

まずSOHO住宅から。仕事場を、個室（私的領域）と外部（公的領域）のあいだの中間領域として位置づけました。外部側、つまり共用廊下側から見ると、玄関前のテラスがあって、玄関扉があり、そこを入ると仕事場です。スタジオと名付けました★12。スタジオの奥は個室や水まわりといったプライベートな空間になっています。スタジオは天井仕上げがなく、デッキプレートに木ルーバーを設けただけの空間です。気積を大きくしたいために天井を張りませんでした。一方、個室や水まわりには天井があります。天井裏を設備スペースに充てると同時に、こぢんまりとした感じをつくりたいと思ったからです。

　スタジオから入って奥に行くにつれて、徐々にプライベートな空間になるわけです。そして、テラスも玄関もスタジオも床レベルはフラットです。このような形式をスタジオアクセスと呼ぶことにします。先に紹介した《写真家のスタジオ付き住宅》は、座位、立位、臥位といった所作に応じた空間配列でした。おなじく職住一体の住宅ですが、

この《食堂付きアパート》のスタジオアクセスは、開放度に応じた配列になっているといえます。

　スタジオと個室とのあいだには3枚引きの引戸を設けているので、プライベートな空間が覗かれないようにもできます。スタジオは玄関側をガラスファサードとしていて開放的なわけですが、夜になって縦型ブラインドを閉じれば、スタジオはリビングのように使うことができます。中間領域としてのスタジオに、視線制御のレイヤーが二重に設けられていることで、時と場合に応じて、スタジオが内向きになったり外向きになったり調整できるわけです。

路地
路地は看板や植栽を置く場所だったり、休憩場所だったりする。
Alley
The alley could be used for a sign or as a recreation spot.

スタジオ
スタジオは仕事場にも使える。幅があり、四角い部屋なので家具のレイアウトがしやすい。
Studio
The studio is large, making it easy to lay things out.

プライベート空間
奥に位置し、引戸でプライバシーを調節できる。
Private space
Positioned in the rear, the bright private space abuts the outside. The fittings can be arranged to partition this space and the studio.

SOHO住宅平面図 1:150
SOHO unit plan 1:150

I started with the SOHO units, positioning each workspace as an intermediate area between the bedroom and bath (private area) and the outdoors (public area). The latter consists of a common passageway, a terrace outside the entrance, and an entry door leading into the workspace, which I call the studio. ★12 To the rear of the studio is a private area consisting of a bedroom and bathroom. The studios do not have finished ceilings, but only wooden louvers suspended from deck plate; I left out the ceiling to maximize the cubic space of the studio. The bedroom and wet area, on the other hand, are ceilinged to provide storage space for equipment as well as a cozier ambience.

As one proceeds toward the rear of the studio, the space becomes increasingly private. The floors of the terrace, entrance, and studio are all at virtually the same level, in a "studio-access" format. In the "Photographer's House with Studio" I introduced earlier, I arranged the spaces according to the postures of sitting, standing, and relaxing. Though the "Apartments with a Small Restaurant" plan was for a similar live/work residence, the studio-access format could be said to arrange its spaces according to their degree of openness.

Between the studio and the bedroom I placed three sliding doors, ensuring that the private area is not exposed from the front. The studio entrance consists of a glass façade, giving the workplace an open atmosphere. At night, however, vertical blinds can be drawn to make the studio feel like part of the living space. Placing these two visibility-limiting layers in the studio allows it to function as an intermediate area that can be either interior- or exterior-oriented depending on the time of day or the occasion.

★12
靴の脱ぎ履きの問題については試行錯誤しました。仕事場であるなら下足スペースとすることも考えられましたが、少人数の仕事場であること、職住一体の空間であることから、スタジオは上足のスペースとしました。玄関床は、幅は部屋の幅いっぱい、奥行きは80cmとして、エンボス加工の施された長尺塩ビシートで仕上げています。この玄関とスタジオの床レベルは3mmの段差しかなく、事実上、フラットです。玄関床がそれほど必要ない場合も想定し、家具レイアウトの自由度を確保しようと考えたからです。

Resolving the question of where to put on and remove one's shoes took some trial and error. Since the studio was a work area I considered making it a space where shoes are worn, but decided against it since the studio is to be occupied by a very small number of people and is, after all, a live/work space. The *genkan* entry floor extends the entire width of the room, 80 cm deep, and is coated with embossed PVC sheeting. The studio floor is only 3 mm higher, so they are essentially level—something I did to provide more latitude in laying out furniture when a special entry floor is not needed.

スタジオの外側は、玄関前のテラスを介して、共用廊下があります。玄関前テラスには仕事場の看板や植物などが置かれていますが、共用廊下とのあいだには柵などを設けていないため、一見、幅3mほどの路地のように見えます★13。この路地は街路から始まって、ぐるぐると螺旋を描きながら3階にまで至るので、立体路地と名付けました。螺旋状の動線空間としたのは、まず、すべてのSOHO住宅の前を通るように考えたからです。また、立体路地を行き来する過程で、下町の都市空間を歩くような体験をもたらしたかったからです。1階の路地は隣地のお店の脇を通る薄暗い空間であり、2階の路地は隣家や向かいの家とベランダどうしが向かい合うようなすこし明るい空間、3階の路地になれば周囲の木造住宅の屋根の上に出ます。

　立体路地に沿って、各階にシェアファシリティを配置しました。洗濯機や菜園などです。建物全体を貫く立体路地があり、シェアファシリティを必要に応じて使いながら生活するようなイメージです★14。SOHO住宅5戸、およそ8人程度でシェアする規模は、適度な距離感がありつつ、各自が無責任にならないサイズとして適切だと考えました★15。

★13
唯一、境界部分にあるものはといえば、インターホンの付いたポールです。インターホンが玄関の壁に付いていると、玄関扉まで近づくことが常態化します。インターホンポールを玄関扉の手前に立て、必要以上に人が玄関扉に近づかないための物理的な工夫としました。もちろん、そのような作法を共有していることが前提ではあります。
《食堂付きアパート》は毎年のように海外からの視察がありますが、いつもこのインターホンポールについては議論になります。あるときドイツからの建築家は、「人の親切さに頼るところが日本的であるといえるが、ドイツでは現実的でない」と評したので、「風土や習慣を利用することは建築的だと思う」と応えておきました。

The only item that might be called part of an interior-exterior boundary is the pole for each unit's intercom. If we were to attach the intercom to the entrance wall, it would become customary for people to go right up to the front door. By placing it on a pole in front of the doorway, it eliminates the need for people to get too close to the entrance. Of course, this requires some mutual agreement on doorway etiquette.
　People visit from abroad every year to view the "Apartments with a Small Restaurant," and the intercom poles always inspire debate. An architect from Germany commented, "It may be a Japanese trait to trust to the kindness of others, but it would not be realistic in Germany." To this I replied, "I think it's a part of architecture to utilize the customs or culture of the locality."

Outside the studio, beyond the terrace in front of the entrance, lies a shared passageway. Workplace signage, potted plants and the like can be placed on the terrace, and since there is no fence between it and the passageway, the latter has the appearance of a three-meter wide alley. ★13 This alley begins at street level and spirals up a staircase to the third floor, so I dubbed it the "cubic alley." One reason I created this spiral line of flow was so that it would pass in front of every SOHO unit. I also wanted the experience of walking along the cubic alley to conjure up the sensation of walking through a city neighborhood. On the ground floor the alley is a slightly dusky space where it skirts the shop next door; on the second floor it is a bit brighter, facing as it does the verandas of neighboring houses; on the third floor it emerges above the roofs of the surrounding wooden houses.

Along the cubic alley, I placed shared facilities—washing machines, a vegetable garden—on each floor. My image of residents accessing those facilities as needed via this alley passing through the entire building. ★14 With five SOHO units occupied by around eight people, I thought this was the right size for a building that would afford a certain degree of mutual distance yet sustain a sense of shared responsibility. ★15

★14
立体路地には大きな軒が張り出していて、入居者たちによって楽しく使われています。看板や鉢植えを飾ったり、椅子やテーブルを置いて外の居場所にしたり。想定外の使われ方は設計者にとってうれしいことです。写真は軒下でのBBQの様子。キッチンが近いので下ごしらえもスムーズ。階段脇のゴーヤカーテンといい、使われ方に驚きました。

Broad eaves extend over the cubic alley, creating a space that residents enjoy using. They may place signs and potted plants there, or tables and chairs for use as a kind of outdoor living room. Nothing pleases an architect more than seeing one's design put to unexpected uses. The photo shows a barbecue taking place in the space under the eaves. The close proximity of the kitchen makes for smooth preparations. I was surprised by the curtain of gourd vines next to the stairs.

★15
地域社会圏研究会では、ファシリティの種類に応じて適当なシェアのサイズを求めました。その知見が生かされています。(山本理顕ほか『地域社会圏主義 増補改訂版』)

I have applied the findings from our discussions in the Local Community Area Study Group on the appropriate size for shared facilities according to the type of facility. See Riken Yamamoto et al., *Chiiki shakai-ken shugi (zoho kaitei-ban)* (Local Community Area Principles, revised and expanded edition).

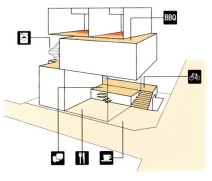

中間領域としての建築的な工夫はほかにもあります。

　たとえばスタジオの中に設けられているキッチンは、幅はコンパクトですが奥行きはゆとりがあります。幅は1.8mとミニキッチンのサイズですが、1階に食堂があるので、住宅内のキッチンは簡素なものと割り切りました。奥行きは68cmあり（このサイズの賃貸住宅なら一般に55～60cm）、それは、SOHOとして使う際に、ミニ冷蔵庫をキッチン下に納められるようにという考えに基づいています★16。その場合、キッチン脇の冷蔵庫置場に複合機を置くこともでき、SOHOとしての利便性がさらに高くなります。

　仕事場を大きく確保するために、水まわりもコンパクトにしています。バスタブはあるものの、基本的にはシャワーを使うことを想定しています。それは、《食堂付きアパート》の近くに銭湯が2軒あり★17、足を伸ばしてお湯に浸かりたければ、そちらに行きましょう、という考えによります。

　仕事場を住宅の中に取り込むというとき、仕事場を使いやすくするために、食堂や銭湯という周辺の生活資源との相対関係のなかで住宅設備のスペックを決めているわけです。中間領域という考え方を採ると、視野を広げたなかで設計を考えることになります。

There are other architectural devices that serve as intermediate areas as well.

For example, the kitchens in the studios are compact but fairly deep. They are mini-kitchen size, only 1.8 meters long, but I determined that a simple kitchen would be adequate for units in a building that has a restaurant on the first floor. Their 68-cm depth (55 to 60 cm is more typical for kitchens in rental units this size) allows a mini-refrigerator to fit under the counter, which I felt should be a consideration for a SOHO unit since it leaves room to install a multifunction printer/copier in the space next to the kitchen where a refrigerator might otherwise go. ★16

To make room for a large workspace, the wet area is also compact. Though it includes a bathtub, the assumption is that the user would mostly shower, particularly because there are two public bathhouses nearby which residents might be encouraged to patronize. ★17

In combining workspaces with residential spaces, I have thus tried to enhance the workspace's usefulness by factoring in the availability of resources in the neighborhood, such as restaurants and bathhouses, when determining the specifications for unit fixtures. Applying the concept of the intermediate area helps to broaden one's outlook in designing such structures.

★16
キッチン下部は、FF型給湯器の設置スペースになっています。《食堂付きアパート》の各住戸には一般的に見られるベランダがありません。ベランダがないと、給湯器や室外機の置場に困るわけですが、奥行きのあるキッチンは設備スペースとしても活躍しています。規定の不燃仕上材を貼るなど、安全性確保はいうまでもありません。なおベランダがないのは、その分の面積を玄関前テラスに当てたからです。つまり玄関前テラスがあるからといって共用部比率が高いわけではありません。

The underside of the kitchen counter contains space for a forced-flue (FF) water heater. Since the units in this apartment house do not have typical verandas, water heaters, air conditioning units and the like cannot be placed outside as is the norm. Therefore I have used the relatively deep kitchen area for such fixtures. Safety is of course ensured by the use of non-combustible materials as required by law. I applied the area normally taken up by a veranda to the terrace outside each entrance. Even so, the percentage of common-use space is by no means high.

★17
多くの銭湯が後継者問題を抱え、そのために廃業に追い込まれるケースが多いようです。幸いクライアントが地域の実情に明るい商店会の元会長だったこともあり、銭湯の代替わりがうまく進みそうな状況を知ることができたため、信頼できる地域資源として設計に反映させたのです。

Many public baths in Tokyo are going out of business due to a lack of successors to take over. Happily, the client is the former chair of the local shopkeepers' association and is well versed in neighborhood affairs. Thanks to an inside tip that the nearby bathhouses were undergoing successful changes of ownership, I was able to incorporate them into my design as reliable local resources.

　さらに、食堂も中間領域であることを強く意識してつくった空間です。SOHO住宅5戸が螺旋状の動線で繋げられてアパートとなっていますが、食堂は、アパートと街の中間領域として位置づけています。その現れとして、出入口はアパート側と街路側の2カ所にあり、床レベルも2通りあります。お客さんがふらりと入ってきやすくするために街路側は地面とフラットで、高天井の空間になっています。そこから90cmほど上がったアパート側はその分天井が低くなり、落ち着いた雰囲気の空間となっています。食堂は10坪と小さいのですが、床レベルの差や対角に設けた開口部の効果によって空間に動きが生まれ、移動のたびに周辺の街の見え方にも変化があるので、広がりを感じさせます。

The restaurant is another space I designed based on a strong sense of its role as an intermediate area. Since this apartment house consists of five SOHO units arranged along a spiral line of flow, the restaurant serves the function of an intermediate area between the apartments and the street. To reflect this function I gave the restaurant a split-level floor with entrances from the apartment side and the street side respectively. To encourage customers to enter, the street-side floor is level with the pavement and has a high ceiling. The floor on the apartment side is 90 cm higher with a concomitantly lower ceiling, which imparts a more intimate mood to the space. The restaurant is only 10 *tsubo* (33 square meters) in area, but the split levels and the apertures at different angles create movement in the space. As one moves through it, one sees the cityscape outside from different angles as well, adding to the overall sense of spaciousness.

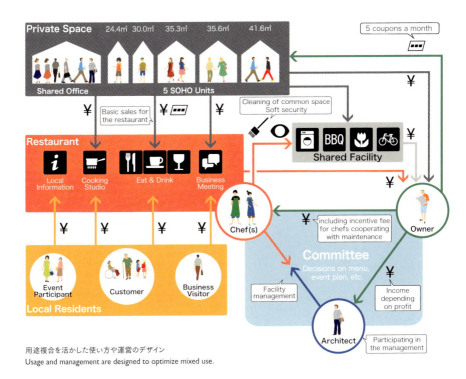

用途複合を活かした使い方や運営のデザイン
Usage and management are designed to optimize mixed use.

　このような作り方をしたうえで、用途複合を活かした使い方のデザインもしました。上階のSOHO住宅の住人や、半地下のシェアオフィスの人たちが、食堂のアイドルタイムに打ち合わせスペースとして使うことができます。食堂の側からしても、準備中であっても勝手を知った人なら居てくれて構わないし、窓に人影が映ればお店のアピールにもなるし、コーヒーを一杯でも頼んでくれさえすれば準備中であってもウェルカムなわけです。中間領域が相乗効果を生むような使い方を引き出しています★18。

　しばしば、「《食堂付きアパート》は、ラーメン屋が１階にあるアパートと何が異なるのか」と聞かれます。ここまで述べた内容ですでに明らかだと思います。食堂はアパートと街の中間領域であり、SOHO住宅の仕事場は私的領域と共用廊下の中間領域です。中間領域として各所を位置づけることによって、複合のメリットを空間化し、時と場合に応じて外向きにしたり内向きにしたり混ぜたりと調整できるわけです。それゆえに、食堂では新旧の住民が分け隔てなく混ざり合い、アパート内には仕事場の雰囲気が漏れ出して、居住者の人となりがそれとなく伝わってくるのです。そしてそのような外向きの意識は、個人の仕事が契機になっているために、自然体で継続的であることが大切です。

Through this design I sought to enhance the mixed-use aspect of the building. For example, residents of the SOHO units upstairs as well as users of the shared office in the semi-basement can use the restaurant as a meeting space during its idle hours between meal times. For the restaurant, having regulars on the premises during off-hours should not be a problem; the sight of customers visible through the windows enhances its appeal, and users of the space can ensure their welcome by ordering a cup of coffee. An intermediate area generates synergistic effects by encouraging such uses. ★18

I often get asked, "So what's the difference between your apartments-with-restaurant and an ordinary apartment house with a noodle shop on the ground floor?" I think the difference is clear from the description above. The restaurant here is an intermediate area between the apartments and the street, and the SOHO workspaces are intermediate areas between the private spaces and the shared passageway. Arranging intermediate areas in this way creates spaces that enhance the mixed-use concept, enabling users to orient them outwardly or inwardly depending on circumstances or the time of day. As a result, old and new residents can mingle in the restaurant, while the atmosphere of the studios wafts out from the apartments, subtly conveying the character of the residents. Significantly, this outward orientation naturally sustains itself because it is fed by the work of individual residents.

★18
この使い方のデザインは、基本設計の途中から描き始め、いろいろな実例を見ては随時更新していました。各用途に当てられる部屋の大きさを、賃料などから求めるための検討にもなりました。
たとえば、設計当初は食堂の位置づけは居住者向けのシェアスペースでしたが、クライアントといろいろな実例を見て学ぶうちに、持続性を考えて、「半開きのシェアスペース」という位置づけとしています。食堂は10坪と小さなものですが、考えようによっては、自分たちで運営することもできる大きさです。大儲けはできないけれど、大損もしない。シェフがひとりで回すこともできそうだ。そんなことから求めた大きさです。ちなみに銀行からは1階全部を飲食店にしたほうが融資額が増えるといわれましたが、テナントを誘致するのも大変だし、失敗したら損失も大きくなるし、そもそも「半開きのシェアスペース」に育っていくのか不安だったために、「小さな食堂」を選択しました。
商店街とともに生きてきたクライアントには、ときどきお店がリニューアルするほうが街への刺激になる、という考えもありました。そこから、将来独立したいシェフが頑張る場所、という発想も生まれました。このインキュベーション的な位置づけは、上階のSOHOにも貫かれています。職住一体として始めた仕事が軌道に乗れば巣立っていく、それを目の当たりにすることがオーナー冥利に尽きる、という考えです。

I began developing this mixed-use design part way through the basic design, altering it as I went along based on various precedents I studied. The size of the rooms for different uses was also adjusted in view of such factors as the rent to be charged.

Initially, for example, the restaurant was to function as a shared space for residents, but after studying a number of examples with the client, we decided to position it as a "semi-public" shared space to enhance its sustainability. Though only 10 *tsubo* in area, its small size makes it feasible for the tenants themselves to manage if they wish. It's not big enough to turn a huge profit, but it will not incur major losses either. The client also wanted the restaurant to be compact enough for one chef to handle alone. The bank, incidentally, said that a larger loan could be obtained by turning the entire ground floor into a restaurant. That, however, would make it difficult to attract tenants, and the risk of losses would be higher. Given the uncertainty attendant upon cultivating a semi-public shared space there from the outset, the client decided on a small restaurant.

Having made a living as part of the local shopping district, the client felt that occasional renewal of the shops had a stimulating effect on the area. From that emerged the idea of having a place where a chef with aspirations to eventually open his own restaurant could hone his skills. This notion of a place for incubation also extends to the SOHO units above. Nothing would make the owner happier if people starting out in these live/work spaces eventually do well enough to strike out on their own.

プロジェクト・コラム ❶ 《緑町の集合住宅》

Midoricho Housing

　《緑町の集合住宅》は旗竿敷地に建つ2階建ての長屋です。オーナー住宅と賃貸住宅2戸の3戸からなります。賃貸住宅は未就学児のいる子育て世帯向けを想定してつくられています。各住宅は小さな仕事場を持っていて、《食堂付きアパート》と同様に、スタジオアクセスの形式を採用しました。オーナー住宅のスタジオは時おり近隣に開放され、「住み開き」を実践する場所になります。

　ここでは、各住戸をメゾネット形式にして、寝室や水まわりは2階に持ち上げ、1階には外部空間と関係を持ちやすい諸室のみを配置しました。接地型のスタジオアクセス形式のひとつのバリエーションです。旗竿敷地の竿にあたる外部空間が、この3戸だけでなく、手前側の隣家とも関係を持てるようになることを期待しています。

　賃貸ユニットの専有面積は40㎡ですが、未就学児を想定するのであれば子ども室が不要であるため、個室はやや大きめの1室のみとしています。賃貸住宅の居住者は、住宅ローンが組みにくくなる40歳までというのがひとつのパターンですが、一方で、東京における初産平均年齢は32.3歳（母親）です。つまり、賃貸住宅に住み続けるのは、子どもの年齢が7歳前後までが多いという計算になります。このような分析から、子ども部屋を別に用意しなくてもよいとし、むしろ1室だが大きめの個室を確保することとしました。

"Midoricho Housing" is a set of three two-story townhouses—the owner's home and two rental units—on a flag-shaped lot. The rental units are designed for small families with preschool children. Each residence has a small workspace in a "studio-access" format like that of the Apartments with a Small Restaurant. The studio attached to the owner's residence can be shared by the tenants, thus supporting a community of weekend carpenters and child rearers.

These apartments are maisonette or duplex units with sleeping quarters and wet areas on the second floor and only rooms amenable to contact with the outdoors placed on the ground floor—in short, a variation on the ground-level studio-access format. My anticipation is that the outdoor space that forms the "pole" of the flag lot will facilitate interaction not only among the three units, but with their neighbors as well.

The exclusive area of each rental unit is 40 square meters. Since a preschool toddler should not require a separate bedroom, each unit has only one, relatively spacious bedroom. Residents of rental units are typically under 40, the age when it becomes more difficult to obtain home loans in Japan—but at the same time, the average age at which women have their first child is 32.3 in Tokyo. Thus most couples tend to rent until their first child is around seven. From this analysis we determined that a separate child's bedroom would not be necessary as long as the single bedroom was on the roomy side.

断面図 1:200
Cross Section 1:200

UNIT 1　UNIT 2　UNIT 3

2階
2F

1. 路地庭　Alley
2. スタジオ　Studio
3. キッチン　Kitchen
4. カスタムルーム　Custom room
5. ラウンジ　Lounge
6. 個室　Private room

1階平面図 1:200
1F plan 1:200

I-4　内発的な営みの場——《小商いの実験室》
A Place for Spontaneous Activity: Small Business Laboratory

　〈小さな経済〉の空間は住宅の近傍につくられることもあります。この《小商いの実験室》は、マンモス団地の空き店舗を使ってつくられた、住民たちが趣味や特技を展示し、交換する場です。

　URみさと団地は9,000戸もの住宅を擁し、全国で高島平団地(10,170戸)に次ぐ大規模団地で、15,000人ほどが住んでいます★19。1973年の供用開始からすでに45年以上が経過しており、居住者の入れ替わりもスムーズに進んだことで世代的な多様性があります。また、国籍も多様です。つくばエクスプレス沿線で、大学キャンパスが近いことから、外国人研究者家族が多数住んでいるそうです★20。

　そのような多様性を活かしたコミュニティの場として、《小商いの実験室》は株式会社HITOTOWAの荒昌史さんらによって企画されました。団地の空き店舗を活用し、住民の趣味や特技がエネルギー源となって自主的に運営できるようなコミュニティ空間です。

★19
戸数は、みさと団地、高島平団地のどちらも、賃貸と分譲の合計。なお、高島平団地は1972年に完成し、賃貸8,287戸、分譲1,883戸からなります（UR都市機構HP「数字で見るUR都市機構の60年」[https://www.ur-net.go.jp/aboutus/publication/web-urpress43/special2.html]より）。みさと団地の人口は「三郷市町名別世帯数及び人口データ」による（[http://www.city.misato.lg.jp/1167.htm] 2019年1月1日現在）。

Figures for both Misato and Takashimadaira include rental and condominium units. Takashimadaira Danchi, completed in 1972, has 8,287 rental units and 1,883 condominium units. (Unit data is from the UR website page "60 Years of the Urban Renaissance Agency in Figures" [https://www.ur-net.go.jp/aboutus/publication/web-urpress43/special2.html]; Misato Danchi population data is from "Misato City Household and Population Data by District" [http://www.city.misato.lg.jp/1167.htm], January 1, 2019.)

Sometimes there is an opportunity to build "small economies" in residential neighborhoods. This "Small Business Laboratory" made use of a vacant shop in a mammoth housing complex to provide residents with a place to display and exchange the fruits of their hobbies and skills.

With 9,000 residential units, the UR Misato Danchi is Japan's second largest apartment complex after the Takashimadaira Danchi (10,170 units), and has a population of around 15,000.★19 In the 45-plus years since it opened in 1973, Misato Danchi has enjoyed smooth turnover among its residents, producing a generationally diverse community. It also includes people of various nationalities due to its proximity to a Tsukuba Express train station and a number of university campuses, making it a popular place for scholars from abroad to live with their families.★20

Masafumi Ara and his team at Hitotowa Inc. planned the Small Business Laboratory as a community space to be operated autonomously in an empty storefront by residents of the housing complex, utilizing their demographic diversity and the energy derived from their own skills, interests and resources.

★20
三郷市の人口データ（前掲）によると、みさと団地の人口15,355人のうち日本人は14,237人となっています。このことから外国人は1,118人となり、割合は7.3％。この割合は三郷市全体での2.9％（前掲データより算出）を大きく上回ります。なお、日本の総人口に占める外国人住民の割合は1.96％（総務省「住民基本台帳に基づく人口、人口動態及び世帯数」より。2018年1月1日現在）。

According to the Misato City population data cited above, Misato Danchi has a total of 15,355 residents, of which 14,237 are Japanese. That means the non-Japanese population is 1,118, or 7.3% of the total—significantly higher than the percentage of non-Japanese (2.9%) for all of Misato City (figure derived from the data above). Incidentally, non-Japanese residents make up 1.96% of the total population of Japan (from Ministry of Internal Affairs and Communications, "Population, Demographic, and Household Figures Based on Basic Resident Registers," January 1, 2018).

住民の趣味や特技が「固まり」となって現れるような場をつくろうと考え、辿り着いたのは、住民の活動が住民の作品によって囲まれている状態をつくりだすことでした。作品によって大小さまざまな場を囲みつつ、全体の一体感もある状態。そこから、可変性のあるL字棚のアイデアが出てきました。普段は作品の陳列棚として展開し、時にはコンパクトに折りたたんで大きなイベントも行えます。作品と活動とが綯い交ぜになって団地のファサードとして現れてくるといいなと考えたわけです。

　僕たちは丁番によって棚をL字型に組むことにしました。

　まず駅前のIKEAで棚を、ホームセンターでベニヤを買ってきました。ベニヤの背板を打ち付けて補強したうえで、丁番を介して2つの棚を連結しました。ベニヤにはさまざまな色を塗っておき、それぞれの棚が開きかけのカラフルな本に見えるようにしました。このように棚をL字型に組んだのは、まずは転倒しないように、強度的に安定させるためです。が、同時に開きかけの本のように見せることで、そこからいろいろなものが飛び出してくるような、ワクワクする気分を醸し出したかったからです。棚にはキャスターが付いているので、イベント時には畳んで端に寄せることも容易です。

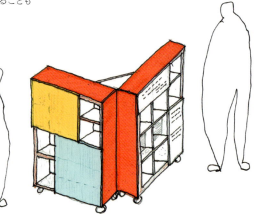

Starting with the idea of creating a space where residents' hobbies and skills would form a "cluster," we arrived at the image of a place where resident activities would be surrounded by their works and products. Depending on the works, they could occupy spaces large or small while also maintaining the unity of the overall space. This approach gave us the idea of L-shaped adjustable shelves, which could stand open as conventional display cases, or fold up into a more compact configuration to make room for special events. Ideally this mix of products and activities would evolve into the "face" of the community.

We decided to use hinges to join shelves together in this L-shape. First we bought shelves at the IKEA store in front of the station and plywood boards from a nearby home improvement center. Nailing boards to the back for reinforcement, we joined the shelves in hinged pairs. With the boards painted in different colors, the shelves resembled colorful, half-open books. The L configuration was for strength and stability, ensuring that the shelves would not fall over. But we also hoped it would spark excited anticipation of what might leap out from the pages of those half-open books. We also put casters on the shelves so they could be quickly folded up and moved out of the way for events.

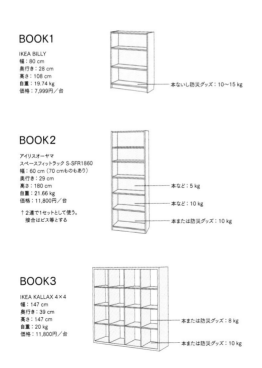

平面図 1:200
Plan 1:200

1. 商店街アーケード Shopping street
2. 小商いの実験室 Small Business Laboratory
3. ユーティリティ Utility

この棚は住民が趣味や特技でつくったものを展示・販売する棚です。1カ月あたり3,000円で借られます。これが思いのほか好評だったとのこと。裁縫や工作でつくったアクセサリーや、刺繍の飾り物などが販売されていました。また、人気の作り手による工作教室が開かれたり、外国人に日本の童話を読み聞かせたり、逆に外国人による料理教室などが開かれたりしていました。

　住民が15,000人もいればさまざまなスキルを持つ人がいるもので、住民のあいだで〈小さな経済〉を回す拠点になっていました★21。回す、というのは、サービスの担い手と受け手とがいつも同じ固定的な関係にあるのではなくて、受け手が時には担い手になりうる、ということです。

　交換しあう場が、コミュニティの本質なのだと思います。交換するものはそれぞれの個性と小遣い程度のお金です。内発的な営みであるがゆえに、イベントを次々に打たなくても済みます。このことは気が楽ですし、等身大の活動のような気がして、健やかささえ感じました。

The purpose of these shelves is to display and sell wares made by residents. They can be rented for 3,000 yen a month. I'm told that they are popular beyond expectation. People sell such items as needlework, handmade accessories and embroidered decorations. Popular artisans hold workshops, storytellers read Japanese children's tales to non-Japanese residents, and non-Japanese residents conduct cooking classes.

A community of 15,000 is bound to include people with a variety of skills, so this space has become a center for the circulation of "small economies" among the residents of the complex. ★21 By circulation I mean that the relationship between service provider and user is not fixed, with people alternating in those roles.

I believe that a place for exchange of this sort is essential to a community. The media of exchange are small amounts of money and the unique attributes of each participant. Because this is a spontaneous, voluntary activity, there is no need to constantly organize events. This makes for a relaxing, healthy environment of "life-size" activities.

★21
《小商いの実験室》の内装工事には、HITOTOWAが募集した住民も参加しました。いわばDIYです。皆が壁の塗装に悪戦苦闘していたとき、通りがかりの老人が手伝ってくれました。聞けば、元塗装職人だとか。一気に場が盛り上がりました。その老人の、まんざらでもなさそうな表情が印象的でした。

Residents recruited by Hitotowa participated in the interior work on this Small Business Laboratory—in other words, it was a DIY project. When the volunteers were struggling to paint the walls, an elderly resident passing by stopped to help. It turned out he was a retired professional painter, and the mood in the space immediately grew brighter. The elderly volunteer's expression of satisfaction was memorable.

プロジェクト・コラム ❷ 《高架下の小商い空間 MA-TO》

Small Economy under Railway

　東京西部の鉄道の駅間高架下に地域コミュニティの場をつくるプロジェクト。シンプルなボックス3棟を高架下の遊歩道に滞留の場をつくるように配置します。うち2棟は幅1間（約1.8m）の個室を11室含む店舗棟で、ちょっとお店をやってみたい地域住民や、アトリエや趣味の部屋を持ちたい地域住民が借りることになり、残りの1棟はシェア工房やシェアキッチンとなっています。

　趣味や特技が高じてセミプロ級のスキルを持つ地域住民たちが、スキルの披露・交換・やりがいなどを求めて集う、そんな場を高架下という屋根付き外部に展開します。

　プレファブメーカーによるユニットシステムが前提で、仲建築設計スタジオにて、建築の配置計画と、インターフェースのデザインを担当しました。

This is a project to build a local community space between stations under a newly elevated railway in Tokyo's western suburbs. Three simple box structures are arranged along a promenade under the tracks to provide rest stops. Two of these consist of a total of 11 small rooms, each about 1.8 meters wide, which are available for rent by local residents who wish to open a small shop or have a studio or workshop for their hobbies. The third building contains a shared studio and shared kitchen. In this way residents with semi-professional skills who wish to display, trade, or otherwise make use of their talents can gather in this unique "outdoor" space with a roof provided by the tracks overhead.

　Predicated on the use of prefabricated units, Naka Architects' Studio is handling the layout plans and interface design for these structures.

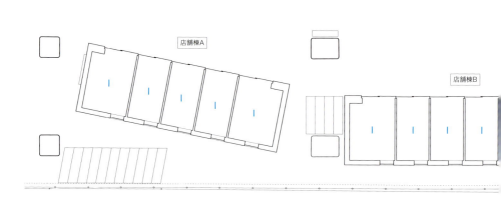

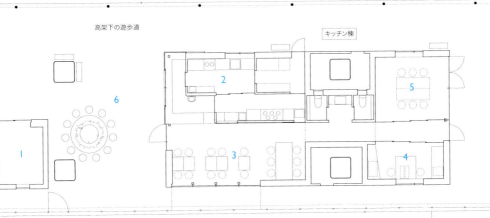

高架下の遊歩道　　　　　　　　　キッチン棟

1. 小商い店舗　Shop
2. シェアキッチン　Shared kitchen
3. フリースペース　Free space
4. シェア工房　Shared workshop
5. 会議室　Meeting room
6. 広場　Plaza

平面図 1:200
Plan 1:200

1–5 顔の見える、外部との交流空間としての中間領域──Socialな循環の可視化
The Intermediate Area as a Space for Face-to-Face Interaction with the Outside: Giving Visibility to a Social Cycle

先に、〈小さな経済〉は諸室の配列と境界要素のデザインに関係する、と書きました。ここまで取り上げたいくつかの事例で、そのことはすでにわかると思います。

生業のあり方が建築のデザインに大きく影響し、そして、地域との直接・間接の関係を左右する、ということですが、それはなぜか。しばらく僕はその理由がわかっていませんでした。

ただ今は、なんとなくこういうことのように思うのです。現代の住宅のほとんどは、サラリーマンの核家族のための居住専用住宅です[22]。居住専用住宅は、外部と関わる理由を、その前提から持っていません。

サラリーマンは通勤をします。仕事場が住宅の外部、それもかなり離れたところにあるということです。生業の場、もうすこし広くいえば、交換の場は、サラリーマンのための住宅の内部にはありません。このような住宅のことを居住専用住宅というわけですが、居住専用住宅は核家族の寝食の場でしかなく、外部と関わる契機を持ちません。地域に対する帰属意識を育むこともありません。ですので、プライバシーの確保のみがその構成原理となるわけです。外観も、そこでの暮らし方も、閉鎖的だとしても不思議ではありません[23]。

[22]
核家族の想定として「標準世帯」があります。総務省統計局では、標準世帯を「夫婦と子供2人の4人で構成される世帯のうち、有業者が世帯主1人だけの世帯に限定したもの」と定義しています。昨今のファミリータイプの住宅供給は、夫婦と子ども1人の3人家族用の2LDKが主流だと思いますが。

There is a "standard household" definition based on the premise of the nuclear family. The Statistics Bureau of the Ministry of Internal Affairs and Communications defines standard households as "limited to four-person households consisting of a married couple with two children, in which only the head of household is employed." However, among family-type housing units available today, the norm would seem to be the 2LDK apartment for couples with one child.

Earlier I wrote that "small economies" affect the design of room layouts and boundary elements. The examples I have introduced so far should bear this out. In other words, how users make their living has a significant influence on building design as well as on their relations, direct and indirect, with the community. But why is this? For some time I did not understand the reason.

Now, however, I think of it in these terms: Nearly all housing in Japan today consists of exclusively residential units for salaried workers and their nuclear families.[22] Such residences have, by definition, no reason to interface with their surroundings.

Salaried workers commute to workplaces outside, and often a considerable distance from, their homes. Residences built for these workers do not contain a place of livelihood—in the broader sense, a place for exchange. This "residence-only housing" is only a place for the nuclear family to eat and sleep, with no occasions for interaction with the outside world, and no need to foster a sense of belonging to the community at large. Thus the only organizational principle is the maintenance of privacy. Both in external appearance and in lifestyle, it is an extremely closed structure.[23]

[23]
こうしてできあがった閉鎖的な住宅が、「核家族という単位が自立的であるべき」という世界観を擦り込む効果を持ったことは厄介なことでした。この世界観にこだわりすぎると、家族規模の縮小が進む状況では、育児や介護といった従来的な家庭機能を誰がどこでどのように担うのか、ということに起因するさまざまな課題が解決できません。

Closed housing of this sort has had the worrisome effect of contributing to the assumption that each nuclear family unit should be autonomous. Excessive adherence to this premise makes it impossible to resolve the many problems that arise from the ongoing shrinking of the family unit, notably the question of where, how, and by whom childcare and eldercare —functions previously handled by the family— should be undertaken.

このような居住専用住宅はしかし、日本において、たかだかこの100年、本格化したのは戦後の70年ほどの歴史しか持たないことも事実です[24]。唯一無二の住宅形式として絶対視する必要はありません。

[24]
第二次大戦前の日本では、農家らの組合施行による土地区画整理事業や、私鉄による沿線の宅地開発がありましたが、そこでどのような住宅が供給されたのか、興味があります。おそらく、多様な住宅形式が供給され、核家族のための居住専用住宅はごく一部であったと理解していますが、どうでしょうか。
鈴木博之はその著書『都市へ』(中央公論新社、1999)において、都市の拡大に伴う宅地開発の2つの流れに触れた後に、大都市近郊であたらしい住居の形式が生まれたとして、サラリーマン層の中廊下型住宅を挙げています(pp.331-332)。中廊下型住宅は、接客の場に重点を置いた間取りと評価されており、また使用人スペースも設けられていたので、居住専用住宅というわけではないようです。
鈴木成文『住まいを読む──現代日本住居論』(建築思潮研究所編、建築資料研究社、1999)では、戦前の住宅について4類型を示していますが(p.12)、居住専用住宅は戦後のモダンリビングを経ながら形成されたとしています(p.14, p.90)。なお本書は、中廊下型住宅の変遷について詳細に述べています。接客スペースと茶の間の位置づけの変化をもとに、接客の形式よりも家族本位を次第に選択していったと述べている点は、居住専用住宅への変化を準備する動きとして興味深いものです(pp.74-75)。
戦前の居住専用住宅の割合はどうであったか。東京市では、1930(昭和5)年には店舗併用住宅は47%でしたが、1941(昭和16)年には商業や工業との併用住宅は23%に減っています(上田篤＋土屋敦夫編『町家──共同研究』鹿島出版会、1975、p.374)。専用住宅が徐々に増え、商売をやめた家は「仕舞屋(しもたや)」と呼ばれました。とはいえ、2013年における東京都内の併用住宅の割合は1.6%(平成25年住宅・土地統計調査結果)ですから、戦前の併用住宅の存在感はかなりのものであったといえます。
なおこの本において居住専用住宅とは、核家族が住むためだけに利用し、交流・交換の場をその内部に持たない住宅、という意味で用いています。

However, it is also a fact that residence-only housing has existed in Japan for at most a century—and for all practical purposes only the seven decades since the end of World War II.[★24] There is no need to treat it as the only viable format for housing in this country.

★24

I am interested in what sorts of housing were available in prewar Japan, when farmers' cooperatives carried out land readjustment projects and private railway companies developed land for housing along their lines. Though I am not sure, my understanding is that a variety of housing formats were provided, of which residence-only dwellings for nuclear families comprised only a portion.

Hiroyuki Suzuki, in his book *Toshi-e* (Toward Cities; Chuo Koron Shinsha, 1999), discusses two trends in residential land development accompanying urban expansion, then cites central-corridor-type dwellings for salaried workers as an example of new residential formats that appeared in the suburbs of the biggest cities (pp. 331-332). The central-corridor format is described as a layout that prioritized spaces for receiving guests as well as for servants, so it does not appear to fit the definition of residence-only dwellings.

Shigebumi Suzuki, in *Sumai wo yomu: Gendai Nihon jukyo ron* (Reading Residences: A Study of Contemporary Japanese Housing; Kenchiku Shicho Kenkyusho, ed., Kenchiku Shiryo Kenkyusha, 1999), describes four types of prewar housing (p. 12), but mentions residence-only dwellings as a product of the postwar "modern living" trend (pp. 14, 90). This same book also goes into detail about changes in the central-corridor residential format. With changes in the role of parlors and guest-receiving areas, people began to choose layouts that prioritized family life over accommodating visitors—an interesting development as it presages the transition to residence-only dwellings (pp. 74-75).

What percentage of prewar housing was residence-only? In 1930, 47% of housing in the city of Tokyo was combined shop-and-residence housing, but by 1941 the percentage of dwellings combined with commercial or manufacturing spaces had fallen to 23% (Atsushi Ueda and Atsuo Tsuchida, eds., *Machiya: Kyodo kenkyu* [Town Houses: Joint Research], Kajima Institute Publishing Co., 1975, p. 374). As residence-only housing gradually proliferated, dwellings that formerly but no longer had businesses on the premises were known as *shimotaya* (lit. "closed shop"). Still, given that combined-use dwellings comprised 1.6% of housing in the Tokyo Metropolitan Area in 2013 (Statistics Bureau, "Results of the 2013 Housing and Land Survey"), such housing could be said to have been a significant presence in prewar Japan.

In this book, I use the term "residence-only housing" to mean a dwelling used only for a nuclear family to live in, with no interior space provided for interaction or interfacing with the outside world.

第二次世界大戦後の日本は、戦災および都市部への人口流入による住宅不足が問題でした。これを解消するため、公営住宅、公団住宅、公庫補助が住宅政策3本柱として整備されました。日本住宅公団が発足したのは1955年で、以来、勤労者向けの集合住宅を供給し続けます。限られた面積のなかで、標準設計——経済合理性のある住戸プラン——がさまざまに検討されました★25。たとえば、東京大学吉武泰水研究室による鉄筋コンクリート造公営住宅51C型は有名ですが、わずか35.5㎡のなかに食寝分離・親子別寝などの理想を叶えようとしたものです。51C型を祖型にした公団住宅55-2DK型はダイニングキッチンをあこがれの的にしました。しかしながら公団が供給してきた住宅には、仕事場も応接間も土間も存在しないことはいうまでもありません。

　時代が下ると住戸プランの模索が始まり★26、そのなかにはコミュニティ形成に寄与するようなプランの模索もあったようですが、居住専用住宅という前提の壁に阻まれたように見えます。

★25
「1951年6月公営住宅法が発布され、"51年度標準設計"では学者・建築家・行政官による標準設計委員会により (…) 一つのアパート住居のパターンが確立される」。「1955年、(…) 日本住宅公団が設立され、(…) 標準設計は公営住宅の計画を担当していた建設省営繕局出身者を主流としてつくられ、それは当然公営住宅の形式を踏襲するものであった」(宮脇檀『日本の住宅設計——作家と作品・その背景』彰国社、1976、p.86)

"The enactment of the Public Housing Act in June 1951 saw the establishment of the '1951 Standard Design' by a Standard Design Committee consisting of scholars, architects, and government officials, [...] thus defining a single pattern for apartment units." [...] "In 1955 [...] the Japan Housing Corporation was established, [...] for which a Standard Design was created by a group consisting mainly of bureaucrats from the Maintenance Section of the Ministry of Construction, which had supervised the planning of public housing. Quite naturally, then, the design followed the format already established for public housing." (Mayumi Miyawaki, *Nihon no jutaku sekkei: Sakka to sakuhin, sono haikei* [Housing Design in Japan: Designers, Works, and Background], Shokokusha, 1976, p. 86)

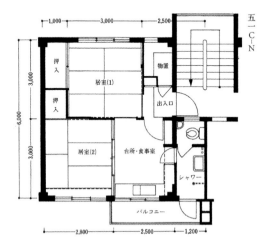

51C-N型。吉武研究室による原案平面
51C-N apartment prototype (draft floor plan by Yoshitake Laboratory).

Postwar Japan suffered from a housing shortage due to the damage inflicted on its cities and the influx of people into them. To ameliorate the situation the central government established three "pillars" of housing policy: public housing run by local governments, public housing run by the Japan Housing Corporation (JHC), and financial assistance from the Government Housing Loan Corporation (GHLC). The JHC has continuously supplied apartment housing for workers since its founding in 1955. From the outset a variety of standard designs for economically rational unit plans of limited area were studied.[25] One famous design is the 51C prototype for ferroconcrete public housing apartments proposed by the laboratory of Yasumi Yoshitake at the University of Tokyo, which fit separate dining and sleeping quarters, and separate bedrooms for parents and children, in a tiny 35.5-square-meter space. The JHC 55-2DK plan, modeled after the 51C, made the dining-kitchen a focus of interest. Needless to say, the apartments provided by the JHC had neither a workspace nor a separate parlor for receiving guests.

Subsequent years saw efforts to devise new housing plans,[26] including those that would contribute to community development, but the premise of residence-only usage continued to be a barrier to innovation.

[26]
「1973年のオイルショックの時代から、公団住宅に対する批判が起きる。(…) 78年以降の公団住宅は標準設計を廃し、ユーザーの需要を配慮し、多様性を旗印とする時代に入る」（渡辺真理＋木下庸子『集合住宅をユニットから考える——Japanese Housing Since 1950』新建築社、2006、p.49）
"Criticism began to be leveled at JHC housing from the time of the 1973 oil shock. [...] In 1978 the JHC abolished standard designs for its housing and began to advertise 'diversity' in designs to accommodate user demand." (Makoto Watanabe and Yoko Kinoshita, *Shugo jutaku wo yunitto kara kangaeru* [Thinking of Apartment Housing in Terms of Units]— *Japanese Housing Since 1950*, Shinkenchiku-sha, 2006, p. 49)

たとえば1983年に建てられた葛西クリーンタウン清新北ハイツ4-9号棟は、リビングアクセスの事例として有名なものです。たしかに共用廊下に面してリビングが設けられ、それまでの公団住宅の構成とはだいぶ異なるように見えます。しかしながら、廊下とリビングは50cmほどの床の段差が設けられ、花台でバッファーがつくられ、プライバシー確保に重心を置いているさまを見て取ることができます。そもそも、リビングによって開くということの必然性が乏しいように考えます。

　ほかにも趣味の部屋としてαルームという部屋を備えた住宅（スクエア玉川上水、1987）が考案されるなど、画一的なプランを打破しようとする実践が続きますが、そのプランを見てもわかるように、住宅内部の幸福のための、オプション的なアイデアです。サラリーマン核家族向けの居住専用住宅という前提が外れない限り、外部と関わる契機はなかなかありません。

　〈小さな経済〉は個人単位で持続的に外部と関わる営みです。その交換のための空間として、僕は中間領域の可能性に取り組んできました。中間領域は、顔の見える、外部との交流空間です。この空間を地域社会のなかに組み込むことができたなら、小さな交換が連鎖し、社会的（Social）な循環として可視化され、今とはまったく異なる風景が現れるはずです。

　さらにいえば、〈小さな経済〉化は情報技術の進展に伴った変化です。会社に行かなくても自宅で仕事ができること、小さな分散的なニーズを束ねて価格交渉力のある仕事にすること、状況を共有しながら任意のタイミングで個々の仕事を進めていくこと、こうした分散しつつも連携しているという仕事の進め方を可能にしているのは、情報技術の進展です。産業革命後の核家族・賃労働を前提にした住宅が居住専用住宅であるなら、〈小さな経済〉のための住宅は歴史的に必然の存在であるように思えるのです。したがって、職住一体の中世社会に逆戻りするというわけでもないのです。

住戸平面図（上階）

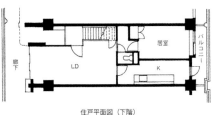

住戸平面図（下階）

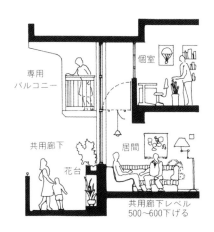

葛西クリーンタウン清新北ハイツ4-9号棟
Kasai Clean Town Seishin Kita Heights, Buildings 4~9.

For example, Buildings 4 through 9 in Kasai Clean Town Seishin Kita Heights, built in 1983, are known for their "living-room access" layouts. Having the living room face the common passageway certainly looks like a major departure from previous public-housing layouts. However, such measures as a 50-cm height differential between the living room floor and the passageway, or setting up flower stands as buffers, demonstrate that priority is given to maintaining privacy, not to opening up the residential space via the living room.

Efforts to make plans less homogeneous can be seen in such ideas as the addition of an extra "alpha-room" to residential units as a space for hobbies (Square Tamagawa-Josui, 1987). But as a look at such plans makes clear, the alpha-room is merely an option to enhance the family's private lifestyle. It is obvious that residences cannot provide opportunities to engage with the community outside so long as they adhere to the model of residence-only housing for commuting workers.

"Small economies" are activities through which individuals engage with the outside world in a sustainable manner. I have explored the potential of intermediate areas as spaces for such interactions.

An intermediate area is, in short, a space for face-to-face interaction with the outside world. If we succeed in inserting such spaces into a local community, the resulting chain of small interactions should manifest itself as a "social cycle" that transforms the environment into something utterly unlike the status quo.

One may add that the proliferation of small economies is a development that follows advances in information technology. IT has made it possible to work at home without commuting to an office; to do work that enhances bargaining power by bundling various disparate, small-scale needs; and to perform multiple tasks under shared conditions but according to one's own choice of timing. If residence-only housing is predicated on the post-industrial-revolution nuclear family and wage labor, then housing for small economies may prove to be a historical necessity for the present era. It does not, in any event, represent a return to the medieval lifestyle of working and living in one place.

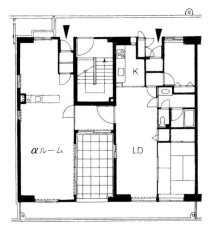

スクエア玉川上水
Square Tamagawa-Josui.

2　自然とともに居ること——Ecologicalな循環

Coexisting with Nature—An Ecological Cycle

2–1 屋根付き外部・地続きの床 ——《白馬の山荘》
A Roofed Outdoor Space with a Ground-Level Floor: Villa in Hakuba

住宅の半分を「外部」にしてみるとどうなるか。《白馬の山荘》はそんな興味から取り組んだ作品です。

　白馬村は長野県北部、北アルプスの麓の街で、オリンピックのスキー会場にもなったように、豪雪や寒さで有名なところです。敷地は村のなかでも標高が高いところにあって、雪は3m近く積もりますし、最低気温は氷点下15℃近くになることもあります。ところが、夏はそれなりに暑く、最高気温が30℃になることもあります。つまり、気温の年較差★27が大きい地域です。敷地は林の中で、夏は下草が茂ることから風も乏しく、また近年は雨が増えているので蒸し暑さを感じることもあります。つまり、冬の寒さや積雪荷重だけを考えて防御的にしてしまうことは簡単なのですが、それだと夏は心地よくない。心地よくないばかりか、山荘を建てるだけあってクライアントは自然の中に身を浸したいわけですから、不適切だと考えました。つまり、冬だけでなく、夏のことも考え併せて建築をつくろうと思いました。

1. 屋根付き広場　Roofed plaza
2. 下の部屋　Lower room
3. バスルーム　Bathroom
4. 書斎　Study room
5. 上の部屋　Upper room
6. 物見台　Lookout

1階平面図　1:200
1F plan　1:200

2　自然とともに居ること──Ecological な循環　｜　72

What happens when we turn half of a residence into the "outdoors"? The "Villa in Hakuba" is the outcome of my interest in this possibility.

Hakuba is a village that sits at the foot of the Northern Japan Alps in north Nagano Prefecture. As befits its selection as the skiing venue for the 1998 Nagano Winter Olympics, the area is famous for its heavy snowfall and low temperatures. Situated at a relatively high elevation even for Hakuba, the villa site gets snow nearly three meters deep and temperatures as low as -15℃. Yet the summers are still hot, with temperatures rising to 30℃. In other words, it is an area with a wide annual temperature range.[★27] The site is in the woods. In the summer undergrowth flourishes and there is little wind; moreover, rainfall has increased in recent years, so it sometimes feels humid. Thus, while it would be easy to simply take defensive measures against the winter cold and snow load, that would make the house uncomfortable in summer. More to the point, such measures do not seem appropriate considering that building a villa in the woods reflects the client's wish to be close to nature. I therefore tried to design a house with both winter and summer in mind.

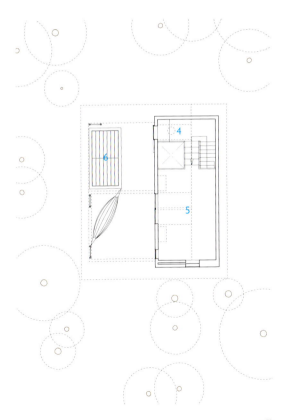

2階
2F

[★27]
気温の年較差とは、一年のうちで最も高い月の平均気温と、最も低い月の平均気温の差を指し、白馬は8月の平均気温が22.6℃、1月が-3.0℃なので、気温の年較差は25.6℃となります。

Annual temperature range indicates the difference between the average air temperatures of the hottest and coldest months of the year. In Hakuba the average temperature is 22.6℃ in August and -3.0℃ in January, for an annual temperature range of 25.6℃.

　この建築は、大きな透明屋根による屋根付き外部空間と地続きの床が特徴です。

　大きな透明屋根は2層分の屋根付き広場をつくります。屋根付きでありながら、その広場の床の明るさは重要だと考えました。そこで屋根には耐久性・耐候性に富む透明なポリカーボネートの折板を用いました。部屋の中から見ると、その明るさゆえに、一見屋根がかかっていないと感じるほどです★28。

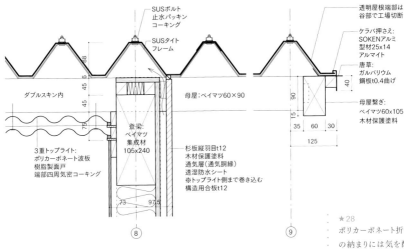

透明屋根断面詳細図 1:10
Section detail 1:10

★28
ポリカーボネート折板屋根の納まりには気を配りました。多雪地帯であることから、折板屋根の汎用ディテールである端部の跳ね上げ納まりとはせず、ケラバ押さえ金物を工夫して端部を閉じる納まりとしました。そもそも跳ね上げ納まりは金物が外観に露出するので見苦しい。また気温の年較差が大きい地域であることから、温度に対する線膨張率が大きいポリカーボネートの留め方にも注意を払っていました。

We paid special attention to the detailing of the folded-plate polycarbonate roof. To deal with the heavy snows of the area, we closed the roof edge with verge-covering metal fittings instead of the raised-edge detailing typical of most folded-plate roofs. Besides wishing to avoid the unsightly exposure of the fittings used in raised edges, we also gave thought to the question of how to fasten down polycarbonate, with its high linear thermal expansion coefficient, in view of the wide annual temperature range of the area.

The design is notable for including an outdoor space with a floor flush with the ground and a large transparent roof overhead.

The transparent double-skin roof turns the space into a large roofed "plaza." To ensure that bright light reaches the floor of the plaza, I used durable, weather-resistant clear polycarbonate folded plates for the roof. From beneath, the light can be so bright that the roof is almost invisible. ★28

　大きな屋根があるおかげで広場には雪が積もりません。そのため、室内の床は地面とフラットにできます。積雪を避けるために、高床式の住宅にしなくてすみます。このことによって、自然との近さ、バリアフリー、そして地熱による天然の床暖房効果を手にすることになりました。雪は氷点下の環境において、断熱材として働きます。だいたい10cmでグラスウール断熱材の1cmに相当します。2〜3mも積もれば、立派な断熱材です★29。住宅の周りはそのような雪が覆っている一方で、住宅の床は地面に接しているので、地熱が効率よく床面に蓄積します★30。それゆえ床の表面温度は外気温よりも断然高く、平均すればプラス10℃ほどに保たれています。たまに訪れる寒冷地の別荘にありがちな、氷のように冷えた床になりません。

　透明屋根は夏冬を通して機能します。住居空間の上の透明屋根の下に、水平剛性を取るための合板でできた屋根面があり、1次止水面を形成しています。つまり、ダブルスキンになっています。これが重要です。

　冬は雪国の軒先にありがちなスガモレを抑制します。ポリカーボネート屋根の上に雪を溜め、ダブルスキン内に外気が通るようにしているので、室内の熱（断熱もしっかりしています）が直接雪を解かすようなことがありません。

　夏はダブルスキン内が60℃もの高温になり、2階の換気天窓を開けることで、温度差換気が行えます。別荘建築は不在時が長く、そのあいだは換気が行いにくく、建築の寿命に関わるという課題があります。透明屋根によるダブルスキンによって、この課題を解決しようとしました。

Thanks to this big roof, snow does not accumulate in the plaza below. Therefore the interior floor can be made flush with the ground outside, because access is not impeded by snow even when it is several meters deep. There is no need to design the house with a raised floor to avoid the snow. This makes several things possible: proximity to nature, barrier-free access, and a natural geothermal floor-heating effect. Snow also functions as heat insulation in below-freezing conditions; a thickness of about 10 cm has an effect equivalent to 1 cm of glass-wool insulation. An accumulation of two to three meters of snow provides excellent insulation.[29] When the house is surrounded by snow at this depth, its flooring, being flush with the ground, can efficiently store geothermal heat.[30] Consequently the surface temperature of the floor is markedly higher than the ambient air temperature by an average of +10 ℃—a far cry from the ice-cold floors of typical villas built in regions with cold winters.

The transparent roof serves a function in both summer and winter. Under the part of the roof that covers the living space is a plywood roof surface, providing horizontal rigidity as well as a primary waterstop layer. This double-skin structure is crucial. In winter it prevents snowmelt leakage from the eaves, a common problem in snow country. The snow accumulates atop the polycarbonate roof, while outside air passes between the two double-skin layers, preventing interior heat from directly melting the snow (there is also ample insulation in place).

In summer, when the temperature inside the double skin rises as high as 60℃, skylights on the second floor can be opened to provide temperature-difference ventilation. Villas are vacant for long periods during which it is difficult to keep them ventilated, which can affect the life of the structure. The double skin of the transparent roof solves this problem.

★29
雪の断熱性を定量的に把握するのはじつはタイヘン難しい。雪の状態や気温によって異なるからです。僕も完全には理解しきれていないのですが、概算という前提で比較すると……
ぬれ新雪：比重 0.1g/cm³ のとき熱伝導率 0.04～0.10[W/(m・K)]
しまり雪：比重 0.3g/cm³ のとき熱伝導率 0.10～0.30[W/(m・K)]
※建築基準法の多雪地域での比重
高性能グラスウール 32K：熱伝導率 0.035[W/(m・K)]
この比較から、白馬の山荘の周りの雪の熱伝導率は、グラスウールのだいたい 3～10 倍程度といえます。
(佐藤篤司「積雪中の熱と水分子の移動」[https://ci.nii.ac.jp/els/contentscinii_20190205162052.pdf?id=ART0008050245] を参考)

It is actually quite difficult to quantitatively ascertain the insulating properties of snow, which vary with the air temperature as well as the condition of the snow. Although I don't fully understand the science behind it, here is a rough comparison:
New wet snow: thermal conductivity of 0.04–0.10[W/(m K)] for a density* of 0.1 g/cm³
Compacted snow: thermal conductivity of 0.10–0.30[W/(m K)] for a density* of 0.3g/cm³
* Densities in heavy-snowfall regions, according to the Building Standards Law
High-performance glass wool 32K: thermal conductivity of 0.035[W/(m K)]
This comparison suggests that the thermal conductivity of snow around the villa in Hakuba is about 3 to 10 times that of glass wool. (Reference: Atsushi Sato, "Heat and Water Molecule Movement in Snow Cover" [https://ci.nii.ac.jp/els/contentscinii_20190205162052.pdf?id=ART0008050245])

★30
地中では、深くなるにつれて温度変化が緩やかになります。一般に地中深さ 8～10m 程度で、その土地の平均気温に近づくとされます (地下水の有無によって多少異なる)。

The deeper one goes in the ground, the more moderate the change in temperature. It is said that the temperature at a ground depth of 8 to 10 meters approaches the average air temperature of the site (allowing for differences depending on the presence or absence of ground water).

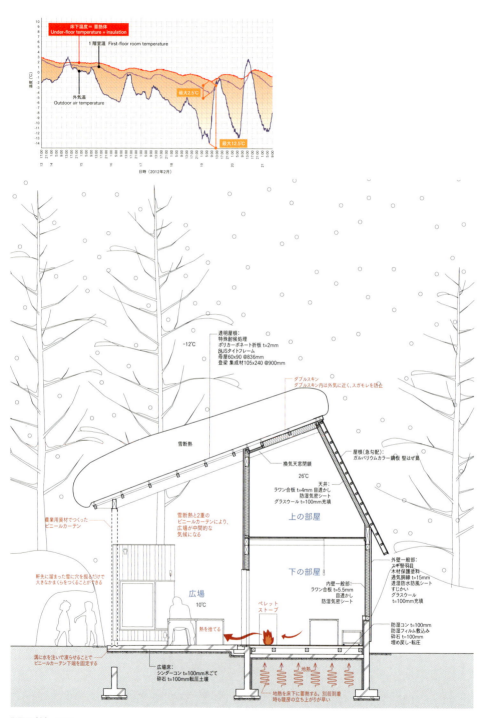

断面図（冬） 1:100
Section (winter) 1:100

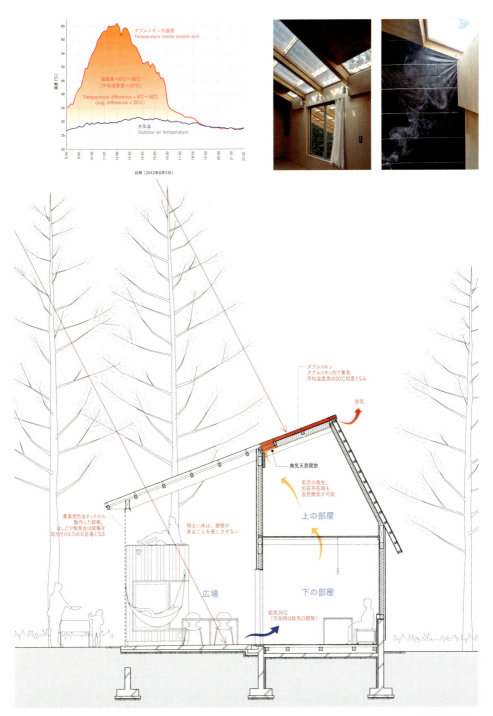

断面図（夏） 1:100
Section (summer) 1:100

2 Coexisting with Nature — An Ecological Cycle

　屋根付き広場は衣替えをします。夏は蚊帳を広場の周囲にぐるりと掛け、ハンモックで眠ります。森の中だけあって、驚くほど大きな蛾がいるので、これは必須です。

　冬はビニールカーテンを掛ければ、薄日が差す日ならトレーナーだけで過ごせる場所になります。すきま風を防ぐために、ビニールカーテンの裾は氷で封着します。カーテン直下の土間コンクリート床に幅30mmの溝を設けました。そこにカーテンの裾を入れて、水を流し込みます。30分も経てばカチコチに凍り、カーテンの裾はガッチリと固定されます。このように氷を使って固定することを「氷封」と名付けました。溝の断面形状は半円形にしています。凍るときに体積が増えるので圧力を逃がして、溝が破損しないようにするためです。軒先のすぐ外側には雪が背丈よりも高く積もっています。雪止めの板を外して、屋根付き広場側から横穴を掘れば、どこまでもかまくらをつくることができます。雪に浸るような生活。

    The roofed plaza changes its wardrobe with the seasons. In summer it is covered with mosquito netting, allowing residents to sleep outside in hammocks. The netting is necessary mainly because of the extraordinarily large moths that dwell in the surrounding woods. In winter, a vinyl curtain transforms the plaza into a space where one can relax wearing nothing thicker than a sweatshirt. If any snow blows inside, even a little sunlight will melt it right away. To keep cold air out, the bottom of the curtain is sealed with ice. I have cut a 30-mm wide groove in the concrete floor directly under the line of the curtain; if one inserts the bottom edge of the curtain in this groove and pours water in, it will freeze stiff inside of 30 minutes, sealing the curtain tight against the ground. I gave the name "ice-sealing" to this method. In cross-section the groove is shaped like a semicircle so as to prevent damage from the pressure of the water's expanding volume when it freezes. Just beyond the edge of the eaves the snow piles up higher than a person's head. If you remove the snow guard boards and start digging laterally from the roofed plaza, you can dig a snow house as large as you like. One can spend the winter here literally in the snow.

夏はダブルスキンの透明屋根で日射を換気の動力に変えたり、冬はその屋根の大きさゆえに床を地面に沈めて地熱を得たり、1年を通じて、自然現象の循環のなかにこの建築は位置づけられています。

　この循環は、「地面」が周期的に上がったり下がったりする様にも見てとれます。冬は背丈よりも高い雪に埋もれ、春に向けてその高さは徐々に下がっていき、やがて下草のない本当の地表面が現れます。夏にかけて下草がどんどん茂り、広場はそれによって再び囲まれた感じになります。秋になって葉が落ちるとアイレベルでは透過性が復活し、そのうちにまた雪が降り始める……。四季を通じて、まるで地面が満ち引きしているような感覚を味わうことができます。

　このような自然現象の循環のことを「Ecologicalな循環」と呼ぶことにします。「Ecologicalな循環」を体感できる空間が、屋根付き広場という中間領域です。衣替えという仕組みによって、この中間領域での快適性を微調整していることもポイントです。中間領域を介して、その地域の「Ecologicalな循環」を理解する。自然とともに居る生活って、こういうことなんだろうと思うのです。

This house exists in the midst of a year-long cycle of natural phenomena. In summer the double-skin transparent roof transforms solar radiation into a ventilation engine; in winter the size of the roof allows the floor below to sit flush on the ground so that it absorbs geothermal heat.

One might say that this cycle entails the periodic "rise and fall" of the ground surface. In winter it sinks below a snow cover that grows head-high or more; as spring approaches, this height gradually decreases until we can see the actual ground surface, not yet covered with undergrowth. With summer the vegetation grows higher and higher until the plaza seems once again to be lower than its surroundings. With the falling of the leaves, autumn restores our ability to penetrate these surroundings at eye level, at least until the snow begins to fall again . . . Through the four seasons, we experience the sensation of the ground rising and falling, like the ebb and flow of the tide.

I call this cycle of natural phenomena an "ecological cycle." The intermediate area provided by the roofed plaza is what makes it possible to physically experience this cycle. A crucial point is that one can fine-tune the comfort level of this intermediate area by changing its "wardrobe." The intermediate area gives us an understanding of the ecological cycle of the region. I think that is what we mean when we talk about living with nature.

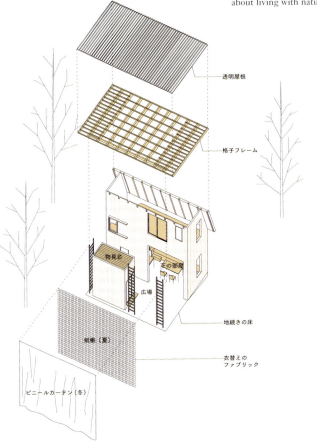

2–2　建築の群れとしての風景 ──《上総喜望の郷おむかいさん》
A Landscape of Grouped Houses: Omukai-san

「Ecologicalな循環」を建築デザインに取り込むということには、降り注ぐ太陽のエネルギーを暖房に利用するような方法も考えられます。日射は屋根に当たって熱に変換され、屋根裏の空気を暖めます。日が沈んで夜になれば、当然屋根裏も冷めることになります。毎日その繰り返しです。その屋根裏の空気が暖かいうちに部屋の中に取りこんで、部屋の中を暖めます。日射エネルギーによる熱をお裾分けしてもらうわけです。

《上総喜望の郷おむかいさん》は、重度の知的障害のある人たちが集まって住む住宅です。このプロジェクトにおいて、日射エネルギーのお裾分け利用に取り組みました。1,000㎡の平屋建なので、屋根の面積も1,000㎡あります。この大きな屋根がポイントです。

18人が3棟に分かれて生活します。1棟あたり6人という、ケアのあり方としてきわめて先進的な小舎制[31]の取り組みです。これら3棟はあいだに共用棟を挟みながら配置しました。全体としては、もともと敷地内にあった木造の住宅（これもまた5人で住むユニット）とあわせて、中庭をつくるようになっています。

★31
ユニットケアに基づいた居住用福祉施設では、そのユニットの大きさが建築計画上重要になります。1ユニットの大きさが12人程度までの場合を小舎制とよびます。
When designing unit-care-based residential care facilities, unit size is a critical factor. Units accommodating up to around 12 residents are referred to as "cottages."

インストールされる機能の種類
Installed functions

色	機能	設備
	屋外ポーチ Outdoor porch	足洗場（特注水栓金具） Footbath (special faucets and fittings)
	ユーティリティ Utility	自火報、メインスイッチ類、キッチン・玄関収納 Automatic fire alarm, main switches, kitchen, entrance
	洗面コーナー Washroom	洗面カウンター、給排水PS Washing counter, plumbing
	ダイニング Dining	暖気利用、 ペンダント照明配線ダクト Warm-air conduits, pendant-lighting wire ducts
	リビング Living	暖気利用、TV、AV機器 Warm-air conduits, TV and audio equipment
	その他（管理諸室） Other (administrative)	暖気利用 Warm-air conduits

One way of incorporating an ecological cycle into architectural design is to use solar energy for heating purposes. When sunlight strikes a roof it is converted to heat that warms the air in the attic space under the roof; then, when the sun goes down, the attic naturally cools, in a cycle that repeats daily. If we bring the attic air into the rooms below while it is still warm, we can heat the rooms—by parceling out the sun's heat, so to speak.

I decided to utilize solar energy in this manner for Omukai-san, a group of residential units for people with severe intellectual disabilities. The entire complex of single-story buildings occupies 1,000 square meters, so the total roof area is about 1,000 square meters too. This large expanse of roof is a key element.

1. 個室　Private room
2. デイルーム　Dayroom
3. スタッフルーム　Staff room
4. 医務室　Doctor room
5. 特浴室　Special bathroom
6. 中庭　Courtyard

全体平面図 1:600
Plan 1:600

　この中庭はとても重要な場所です。元来、福祉施設というものはどうしても内部の機能が重視されるため、外部空間はうまくつくられない傾向にあります。スペースは確保されていても室内との関係に乏しかったり、使われないために空き地のようになってしまったり。ですので、この《上総喜望の郷おむかいさん》は、素敵な外部空間をつくり、そこが日常的な居場所のひとつとなるように考えました。また、中庭があれば、緊急事態が起こったときに、向かい合う棟から職員が気づきやすく応援に駆けつけやすい、といった実用上のメリットもあります。

　外部空間にこだわるのは、知的障害者の住まいをめぐる矛盾[32]をなんとかしたい、という気持ちとともに、そもそも、生活の場に求められる最低限の質を獲得しようと考えたからです。それは、自分の居場所を選択できること。そして天気のいい日も雨の日も外を感じながら過ごすことができ、自然のなかで自分が生かされているような感覚を持てること。言い換えれば、自分を世界のなかに定位することが、生きていくうえでたいへん重要だと考えます。

　そのため、ここではまず個室をきちんとつくり、それらを配置することで中庭をかたちづくりました。中庭は、森羅万象を映す鏡です。樹木が茂り、畑では作物を栽培し、雨の日は川になる凹みが庭を巡っています[33]。

There are three buildings, each housing six people for a total of 18 residents. This cottage-style arrangement of six people to a house is extremely advanced for care facilities of this sort.[31] I arranged the three residences in a semicircle alternating with common-use buildings so that they form a courtyard flanked by an older wooden building on the site, which houses another five residents.

This courtyard is an extremely important space. Typically, care facilities prioritize their indoor functions, so outdoor spaces are given little thought. Even when there is ample outdoor space, it is often poorly connected to the indoors, or falls into disrepair due to lack of use. Therefore I wanted Omukai-san to have an attractive outdoor space that would serve as one place for residents to spend time—in other words, it would become part of their daily lives. The staff also told me that a courtyard surrounded by houses facing one another had the practical merit of facilitating their response to emergencies.

My concern with outdoor space derived from a desire to somehow resolve the contradictions[32] endemic to residences for the intellectually disabled, as well as a desire to ensure a certain level of quality in their living environment. That entails affording residents the opportunity to choose where they want to spend their time, along with a day-to-day awareness of the outdoor environment, thus fostering a sense of living in and being a part of nature on sunny and rainy days alike. Put another way, orienting oneself in the world is a crucial part of being and feeling alive.

To achieve this objective, I first focused on the design of the private rooms and their layout, based on which I then designed the courtyard. The courtyard is a mirror reflecting all of creation. Trees flourish, crops grow in the garden, and a shallow gutter that runs around the periphery turns into a little brook when it rains.[33]

★32
上総喜望の郷を運営する社会福祉法人みづき会の樋口敦夫理事長の言葉はたいへん重いものでした。
「街中のグループホームは外部に対して閉鎖的であることが多いのです。周辺住民に迷惑を掛けたくない、という心理が働くためです。しかしそれは、ノーマライゼーションの理念に基づく街中のグループホーム推進の意図が形骸化していることの表れかもしれません。みづき会は、山の中にあるからこそ周辺の自然や集落に親和的な住まいを追求したいのです」。
僕はこの言葉を、建築の本質が生活の場をつくることであり、建築への期待の言葉として受け止めました。

I took to heart the following words by Atsuo Higuchi, chief director of Mizuki-kai, the social welfare corporation that operates the Omukai-san facility:
"Many group homes one sees in the cities are closed to the outside, due to a desire to avoid friction with their neighbors. But that negates the point of building group homes in cities for the purpose of normalization. Precisely because Mizuki-kai is located in the countryside, we want to make it a place that harmonizes with its natural surroundings and with the neighboring community."
I took his words as an expression of his expectations for our design, based on a belief that the fundamental purpose of architecture is to build places where people can live their lives.

★33
皿形側溝を用いた開放型の雨水排水路です。バリアフリー建物において開放型排水路はやっかいな存在なのですが、高橋利彰監督や施工者の協力もあってなんとかかたちにすることができました。底部の一列は工事では仕上げずに残して、みんなで集めたビー玉や石などを混ぜました。施設長の中村敏久さんをはじめ、職員の方々や住人たちがDIYで仕上げました。

The dish-shaped gutter serves as an open rainwater drainage channel. Although an open gutter is a problematic element for barrier-free structures, we were able to create one here thanks to the cooperation of the team of builders headed by Toshiaki Takahashi. We left the bottom of the channel unfinished at the construction stage, then mixed in beads and stones collected by everyone at the facility. It was finally completed by the residents and staff themselves, led by facility director Toshihisa Nakamura.

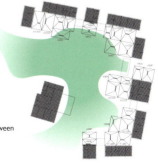

個室と中庭とのあいだの、中間領域としてのデイルーム
Dayrooms as intermediate areas between private rooms and courtyard

2 Coexisting with Nature — An Ecological Cycle

　個室と中庭のあいだは、デイルームと呼ぶ空間です。個室に籠もるわけでもなく、中庭に出るでもなく、なんとなく屋外や他者を感じながら心地よい場所に留まる(時に苦手な人が近づいてきたら離れる)。そんな社会的な空間です。そのためにこのデイルームを次のように定義して、設計を進めました。

- デイルームを個室と中庭の中間領域と捉えること。
- 小さな居場所の集合としてつくること。ただしそれらは隔絶された居場所ではなく、職員にとっても入居者の気配を察知できること。
- 屋根裏の暖気を使った暖房を導入し、中庭に対してデイルームを開放的に維持すること。

Between the private rooms and the courtyard are spaces known as dayrooms. Residents who don't feel like shutting themselves in their room, but also don't want to go outside, can spend time in this comfortable space where they can subtly feel the presence of the outdoors and of other people. (They can also leave if someone they don't like shows up.) The dayroom serves as this social space, which I defined and designed as follows:

- The dayroom should function as an intermediate area between the private rooms and the courtyard.
- It should be designed as a grouping of small "places to be" for residents. However, these places are not isolated, and should lend themselves to observation by the staff.
- The dayroom should be heated by warm air from the attic, and should provide open access to the courtyard.

傘ユニットは、これらを同時に実現するための建築的工夫です。図のように屋根と天井を支える構造材（上弦材と下弦材）が屋根裏を形づくり、傘の柄にあたる部分は細い板状の列柱が並び、これらの列柱のあいだが暖気の通り道になります。列柱の隙間はそれ以外にも、腰高の家具がインストールされて小さな居場所をつくるきっかけになりますし、目線レベルでは視線が抜けるので、ケアする側がデイルームの様子を把握することを妨げません。

　傘ユニットによる屋根の大きさは、一辺4.2mまたは5.6mを基本サイズとしています。1.4mが基本的なモジュールになっているからなのですが、それは個室が幅2.8mスパンでできているためです。2.8mスパンは非常時にベッドのまま避難できるように引き違いサッシの有効開口幅から求めた寸法で、その半分の1.4mがこの建築に通底する基本的なモジュールになっています。

　この傘ユニットの大きさに対して、これらの列柱は華奢に見えるかもしれません。実際に、列柱には方向性があるので、並んでいる方向には揺れます。そのため、隣の傘ユニットは列柱の向きを直交させて配置します。一つひとつの傘ユニットは華奢ですが、それらが複数直結されることにより、安定した大きな屋根になるわけです。そして、列柱がL字型やT字型に並ぶことによって、あちこちに小さなコーナー＝居場所ができます。落ち着いた居場所だけど、孤立していない場所。きわめて短い設計期間で何度も徹夜しましたが、このつくり方を編み出したときはそんな苦労が吹っ飛ぶような発明をした気持ちになりました。

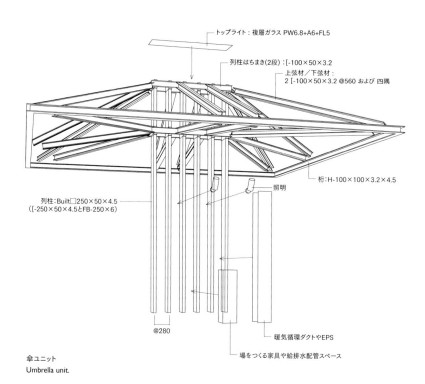

傘ユニット
Umbrella unit.

The umbrella unit is an architectural strategy for achieving all these objectives in one structure. As the drawing shows, the structural elements (top and bottom chords) that support the roof and ceiling form an attic space. The section equivalent to the handle of the umbrella is composed of a row of narrow board-shaped columns, with spaces between the columns serving as ducts for importing warm air. These inter-column spaces can also be used to install furnishings at waist height, thus helping to form "places to be." Also, because they permit a clear line of sight at eye level, the columns do not impede the staff's ability to observe the dayroom.

I designed the umbrella unit roofs in two basic sizes, 4.2 and 5.6 meters on a side respectively. The use of 1.4-meter modules was determined by the 2.8-meter span of the private rooms, a width required to provide apertures with double-sliding sashes to permit the emergency evacuation of residents in their beds. Half that width, or 1.4 meters, therefore served as the basic module for all the structures in this project.

The column rows may appear too slender to support umbrella units of this size. However, the columns are oriented so that they sway in the direction in which they are aligned. I therefore arranged the umbrella units so that the column rows of adjacent units stand at right angles to one another. Although a single umbrella unit may appear fragile by itself, joining several such units together provides a large, stable roof. Moreover, arranging the column rows in L or T formations produces various small corners, i.e. "places to be," that are relaxing but not isolated. It took me many sleepless nights to complete this design in the very short time allotted, but when it was finished I felt the satisfaction of having invented something new.

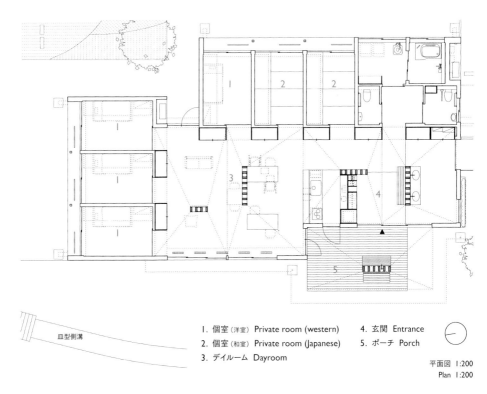

皿型側溝

1. 個室（洋室） Private room (western)
2. 個室（和室） Private room (Japanese)
3. デイルーム Dayroom
4. 玄関 Entrance
5. ポーチ Porch

平面図 1:200
Plan 1:200

傘ユニットの断面方向のデザインは、「Ecologicalな循環」としての暖気利用から決まっています。施設管理上の過度の負担★34を職員に求めることは避けなければいけません。そこで小さく安いファンをタイマー制御付きのスイッチで動かすことにしました。朝晴れていたら、ボタンを1回押してもらうだけです。そうすると、9時〜15時までのあいだの6時間だけ、暖気を取り込みます。そのあいだに得られる太陽エネルギーをマクロで把握し、ファンの風量をもとに必要な屋根裏の体積を求めました。設計時の検討★35では小さなパイプファンで平均高さ100cmの屋根裏があれば、外気温より5.9℃〜11.2℃高い状態で、6時間のあいだ、暖気をデイルーム内に導入できることがわかりました。この検討には、列柱上部のトップライトによる昇温も加味しています。

　問題は、小さな屋根が反復するだけあって、屋根の影が隣接する北側の屋根面に落ちて、効率が下がること。この共食いのような影の影響を抑えるため、南側の屋根は背が低く、北側の屋根は高くなるように、20cmずつの差をつけています。つまり、傘ユニットの屋根裏の高さは、80cm、100cm、120cmの3タイプを設定し、それを南側から順に並べることで、影による悪影響を極力抑えることにしました。

　設計中は試験体を製作して、このシミュレーションとおおむね同じ結果を得ていました。さらに施工中には実物大のモックアップで再度試験をし、屋根裏の温度は予想通り外気より10℃高い状態になりました。

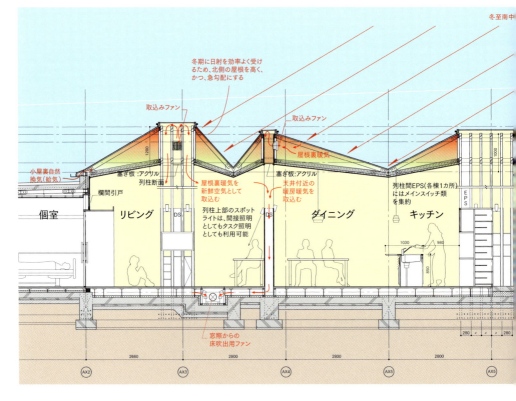

The design of the umbrella units in cross-section was based on utilizing warm air flow per my concept of the ecological cycle. To avoid imposing an excessive management burden ★34 on the staff, I decided to use switches with timers to operate small inexpensive fans. If the weather is fair in the morning, one only needs to push a button once to let in warm air for six hours, from 9 a.m. to 3 p.m. I estimated the amount of solar energy to be obtained during that period, and calculated the required attic volume based on fan air flow. My study ★35 for the design showed that given an attic space of 100 cm average height, a small pipe fan can import air that is 5.9 to 11.2℃ warmer than the air outside into a dayroom for six hours. The study also incorporated additional warming from skylights placed above the column rows.

One problem with this design is that the interation of small roofs reduces efficiency because each roof casts a shadow on the adjacent roof to its north. To reduce this "cannibalistic" effect of the shadows, I designed the roofs so that each one was lower than the roof to its north, with a 20-cm differential between each pair. For this purpose I designed three different attic configurations for the umbrella units, with respective heights of 80, 100, and 120 cm. By arraying these units in sequence from south to north I minimized the adverse effect of the roof shadows.

In the course of the design stage we built a test model that yielded substantially the same results as this simulation. During construction we also built a full-size mockup and ran tests again that demonstrated that the attic temperature was 10℃ higher than the outside air, as predicted.

★34
自然エネルギーを利用するとき、その操作をどうするかにはいつも頭を悩ませます。センサーを巡らせ、電気仕掛けにすれば管理は楽なのでしょうが、イニシャルコストは高くなります。

It is always a challenge to decide how a system that utilizes natural energy should be operated. An electrical system relying on sensors would make management easier, but the initial cost would be high.

★35
設計時はまずモックアップで、屋根裏空気溜まりの温度変化を計測しました。屋根材や下地材を替えながら実験を繰り返し、外気温より10℃高い状態になるような構成にしました。このような実験データを集める一方で、机上シミュレーションでも屋根裏空気溜まりの温度変化を予測しました。実験とシミュレーションの数字を照らし合わせ、ほぼ同程度の数字になることを設計時に把握し、自信をつけながら設計を進めました。

At the design stage we first used a mockup to measure changes in the temperature of dead air space in the attic. After repeated tests with different roofing and substrate materials, we came up with a configuration that achieved attic temperatures 10℃ higher than outside air. In addition to collecting this test data, we also used desktop simulation to predict changes in attic dead-air temperature. Finding as we went along that figures from the tests and the simulation substantially matched, we gained confidence over the course of the design process.

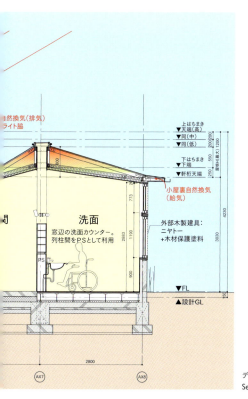

デイルーム断面図 1:100
Section of Dayroom 1:100

2 Coexisting with Nature — An Ecological Cycle

　竣工後に実測したところ、晴れときどき曇りの条件でしたが、屋根裏から取り込む空気の温度は、デイルーム室内温度と比べて、6℃〜10℃高い状態であることが確認できました。また列柱のあいだに板を張ることでダクトの代わりとし、天井付近の空気を窓際の床面から吹くこともしています。コールドドラフトと結露を抑制しつつ居住域空調をするためですが、これもうまく機能しているようです。カーテンを開けて窓際に佇む住人の姿を見ることができます。

　小さな居場所をつくること、それから、連結することで強くなるような構造形式、これら2つの秩序に基づいて、屋根はその勾配に列柱の向きの多様性が映し出されました。一方で高さ方向は太陽エネルギーの循環を利用するための形態的秩序が投影されています。すこしランダムで、しかしごちゃごちゃでもない。「Ecologicalな循環」に着目することで、隠れた秩序に支えられた群れとしての風景をつくりだせたことは、僕にとって大きな驚きでした。

After construction was completed, measurements showed that under partly cloudy weather conditions, the temperature of air imported from the attic was 6 to 10°C higher than room temperature in the dayroom. Also, by placing panels across the column rows I was able to build ducts that carry air down from the ceiling area and blow it out at floor level near the windows. This proved to be effective as a means of regulating living area temperatures while reducing cold drafts and condensation. Residents can be seen spending time near the windows with the curtains open.

Designed according to two organizational principles—creating a group of small "places to be" and joining them together to form a robust structure—these units have roofs with pitches that reflect the varying orientations of the column rows below. At the same time, the orientation of the roof heights reflects an ordering principle based on utilization of the solar energy cycle. The result is a configuration that appears a little random, but not chaotic. I ended up creating a landscape of housing units sustained by a hidden order derived from the ecological cycle, an outcome that came as a big surprise to me.

2–3 流れのなかに場をつくる——《深沢の住宅》
Creating Places in a Flow: House in Fukasawa

風は、ここまで取り上げてきた雪や日射に比べると局地的な条件に左右されやすく、周期や循環を感じにくいものかもしれません。とはいえマクロな視点に立てば、たとえば東京や神奈川であれば、夏の卓越風は南から、冬は北から吹くといった具合に、周期的な傾向はもちろんあるし、気圧の差によって風が吹く以上、地球規模での循環といえます。「Ecologicalな循環」として風を取り上げる場合、建築レベルのスケールでは、（循環というよりも）ある方向性を持った流れのなかに建築を置くことになります。

　日射を適切に遮蔽しながら風の来る方向に開口を開けること。古くからの建築の所作です。一歩進んで、その風をすこしデザインできないか。そのときにどのような建築を構想できるか。そんなことを考えてつくったのが、《深沢の住宅》です。

　敷地は東京都世田谷区の住宅地にあり、南側と東側で道路に面する角地です。敷地は角で大きく角切りされていて、ここに正方形のファサードを立ち上げることを考えました。緩やかな坂を上って近づいていく際に印象的だと考えたからです。

　敷地いっぱいにがらんどうの箱を置き、角に向かって2層吹き抜けの高さを持つ「吹き抜けテラス」を設けました。くじらが大きな口を開けるように、南からの風を最大限に取り込むものです。一方で夏期の日射遮蔽を考慮して、吹き抜けテラスの奥行き寸法を決めています。その正方形のファサードには「グリーンルーバー」を設け、日射を制御するとともに、住み手の人となりを表すインターフェースとしています。お向かいの敷地に立派な桜があり、それを景色として取りこませてもらう代わりに、こちらもなにか景観的に役立つものを提供できるといいなぁと考えたのです。

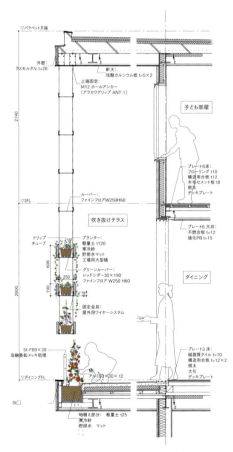

吹き抜けテラス断面詳細図　1:60
Section detail of atrium terrace　1:60

Compared to phenomena like the snow and sunshine I have discussed so far, the wind is easily affected by local conditions and not something one associates with cycles or circulation. From a macro perspective, however, one can see that wind is indeed cyclical on a global scale. Wind is generated by differences in air pressure, which follow cyclical patterns. So in Tokyo or Kanagawa, for example, prevailing summer winds blow from the south, and winter winds from the north. If we treat wind as a type of ecological cycle, then at the level of architecture, we must be aware of placing structures in the midst of a flow that has a certain directionality (rather than a cycle per se).

Since ancient times one architectural strategy has been to open apertures facing into the wind while blocking sunlight. Taking this one step further, we should be able to "design" that wind a bit. What sort of architecture might result? I built the House in Fukasawa with this idea in mind.

The lot is in a residential area of Setagaya Ward, Tokyo. It is a corner lot with streets on the south and east sides. Since the lot is cut off at the corner, I thought of constructing a square façade that would make an impression as one approaches it by climbing up the gentle slope of the street.

I placed a hollow box on the lot that filled the entire site, and added a two-story "atrium terrace" facing the streetcorner. Like a whale opening its spacious mouth, this terrace takes in wind from the south to the maximum extent possible. I established the depth of the terrace in consideration of the need to block out sunlight during the summer months, and laid "green louvers" across the square façade. These not only regulate sunlight but also provide an interface that reflects the character of the residents. The facing lot boasts a beautiful cherry tree; in exchange for enjoying that scenery, it seemed appropriate for this house to also provide something appealing to look it.

グリーンルーバーは、建築化されたプランターです★36。エディブルプランツを育てたり、道行く人の目を楽しませる花を植えたり、住み手の関わりによってその表情がつくられます。夏期においては、日射制御によって室内の熱負荷を抑制し、家の中に多少なりとも涼しい風を取り込もうとしました。土や植栽の蒸散効果によって、ルーバーそのものが高温化することは緩和されます★37。風にそよぐ植物、いわば風の可視化によって、視覚的な涼感も得られます。冬には、沢山の日射が室内まで届き、蓄熱性の高い濃色のタイルが暖かさを蓄えます。

★36
開口幅5mに対して亜鉛メッキ処理された鋼製床材既製品を掛け渡し、その床材の上にプランターを載せています。植物を含めて日射遮蔽要素となります。縦に入るワイヤーはたわみ防止用。
I laid premade planks of galvanized steel flooring across the 5-meter wide aperture and placed planters atop the planks. The plants provide additional solar shading. Vertically hung wires prevent flexure.

★37
壁面緑化の既往研究によれば、壁面緑化の「葉」そのものが気温を下げることはなさそうです（成田健一「緑のカーテンは周囲空気を冷却化するか?」[http://leo.nit.ac.jp/~narita/profile/paper/ceis2009-midoriK2.pdf]）。
一方で、壁面緑化は日射遮蔽による熱負荷の低減、外壁面温度の低下による熱放射の低減、蒸散による顕熱フラックスの低減効果が大きいことが明らかになっています（鈴木弘孝「壁面緑化による温熱環境改善効果」[http://www5.jiu.ac.jp/books/bulletin/2015/env/02_suzuki.pdf]、三坂育正ほか「壁面緑化の蒸散効果に関する研究」[http://leo.nit.ac.jp/~narita/profile/paper/2005CEIS_wallgreen.pdf]）。
もちろん、緑化面積や壁面緑化基盤材の納まりなども関係しますから、《深沢の住宅》が熱的効果において最適化されているわけではないと思います。
Previous studies of wall greening suggest that the leaves of plants themselves do not contribute to reduced air temperatures (Ken'ichi Narita, "Does a Green Screen [Wall Greening Plants] Cool the Ambient Air?" [http://leo.nit.ac.jp/~narita/profile/paper/ceis2009-midoriK2.pdf]).
　However, it has been shown that wall greening has the significant effects of reducing heat load through solar shading, reducing thermal radiation by lowering the temperature of the exterior wall surface, and reducing sensible heat flux through transpiration (Hirotaka Suzuki, "The Thermal Environment Improvement Effects of Wall Greening" [http://www5.jiu.ac.jp/books/bulletin/2015/env/02_suzuki.pdf]; Ikusei Misaka et al., "The Study of Transpiration Effects for Thermal Environment by Wall Greening Plants" [http://leo.nit.ac.jp/~narita/profile/paper/2005CEIS_wallgreen.pdf]).
　Needless to say, such factors as the greening area and the wall greening base material are also relevant. In that respect the House in Fukasawa cannot be said to achieve optimal thermal efficacy.

Green louvers consist of planters employed as an architectural element.[36] They can be used to grow edible plants, or flowers pleasing to the eyes of passersby; their appearance is determined by the residents. The objective of the louvers is to reduce the indoor heat load by controlling sunlight as well as admitting at least a bit of cooling breeze into the house. The transpiration effect of the plants and soil mitigates the heating of the louvers themselves.[37] The rustling of the plants gives form to the wind, adding a visual element to the sensation of coolness. In winter, plenty of sunlight enters the interior, where its warmth is retained by heat-absorbing dark-colored floor tiles.

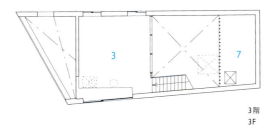

3階
3F

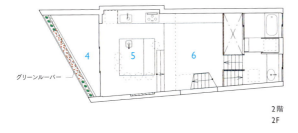

2階
2F

1. ピロティ　Piloti
2. スタジオ　Studio
3. 個室　Private room
4. 吹き抜けテラス　Atrium terrace
5. ダイニングキッチン　Dinning kitchen
6. リビング　Living room
7. ロフト　Loft

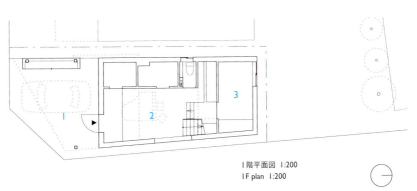

1階平面図　1:200
1F plan　1:200

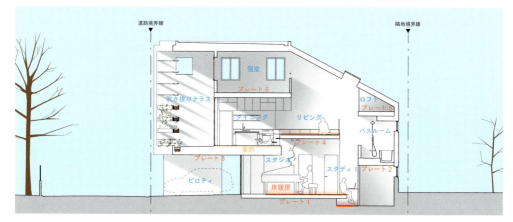

断面図（冬）1:200
Section (winter) 1:200

　がらんどうの箱の中には6枚のプレートを浮かべます。プレートは居場所です。腰壁や手摺によって、流れのなかの淀みのような居場所が生まれることをイメージしました。吹き抜けテラスからグリーンルーバーを経由した風が流れ込み、プレートのあいだを抜けて室内の隅々まで行き渡ります。
　プレートにはそれぞれ異なる素材と性能を与えています。テラスとダイニングには夏の冷感や冬の蓄熱性を兼ね備えた磁器質タイルのプレート、優しい肌触りと床暖房の暖かさが心地よく、ピアノの音を柔らかく吸音する木のプレート、水まわりの清潔感をつくりだすモザイクタイルのプレート、地中に身を沈めるような落ち着きをもたらすモルタルのプレートなどです。がらんどうの箱を通り抜けていく大きな風の流れのなかに、これらのプレート群に挟まれて特徴を持ったいくつもの場所を生み出そうとしました。そしてその風は吹き抜けテラスによって、涼しく感じたり、目に楽しげに映ったりというように、デザインされているわけです。

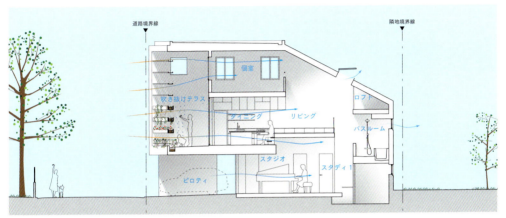

断面図（夏）1:200
Section (summer) 1:200

    This hollow box is filled with six plates, each one serving as a living place. My image is of waist-high walls or railings forming quiet pools of living space amid a flowing stream. The breeze blowing through the green louvers flows in from the atrium terrace, passing among the plates to every corner of the interior.

    Each plate is made of a different material with different properties. The plate for the terrace and dining area uses ceramic tile that provides a cool sensation in the summer and stores heat in the winter. The plate for the piano room uses wood to gently absorb the sound of the instrument; the plate for the wet area uses mosaic tile for a fresh, clean ambience; another plate is made of mortar to give one the sense of nestling cozily into the earth. I wanted to create several places, each with its own unique character, in between these plates amid the grand stream of air flowing through this big open box. The house is designed so that the breeze entering from the atrium terrace becomes a cooling, soothing entity, pleasing to the eyes as well as the skin.

2–4　温熱環境的な中間領域 —— Ecologicalな循環の可視化
Intermediate Areas as Thermal Environments: Making the Ecological Cycle Visible

「Ecologicalな循環」をめぐる建築の実践を紹介してきました。それらは、雪、地熱、太陽の日射エネルギー、風といった自然の要素を用いようとして、その結果、建築の形態的な特徴を導いたものでした。そして、循環する自然の要素を受容し、利用する場所として、いずれも、温熱環境的な中間領域が出現していることに気がつきます。

実践	循環要素	受容の場所	循環に対応する工夫	得られる効果
《白馬の山荘》	雪・地熱	屋根付き広場	衣替え	地表面の満ち干きを感じる
《上総喜望の郷おむかいさん》	太陽日射	デイルーム	屋根の群れ	外部へ開放していても暖かい
《深沢の住宅》	風	吹き抜けテラス	グリーンルーバー	涼風・エディブルプランツ

　この中間領域が呼び水となって、心地よいから外部に開く。たとえば《白馬の山荘》では、屋根付き広場は完全な外部よりはマイルドな空間で、そこから眺める森の様子はいつも新鮮です。屋根付き広場では地表面が満ち干きしているような感覚が味わえると述べました。寒くても暑くても外が気になるし、発見がある。お風呂を屋根付き広場内の「離れ」としてプランニングしているので、外を気にする機会が否が応にも増えます。《上総喜望の郷おむかいさん》では、デイルームはガラスを多用していても暖かく、中庭をいつも意識するような生活になっています。《深沢の住宅》の吹き抜けテラスは、植物を育てるという楽しさを伴った中間領域になっています。

　温熱環境的な中間領域は、「Ecologicalな循環」を映し出す空間といえます。ここでは、自分が自然とともにあることを理解することになります[★38]。

★38
人間のほうが環境に適応していかねばならない半屋外環境では、屋内環境に比べて熱的快適性の受容度が広がることが、中野淳太氏(東海大学准教授)の研究で明らかになっています(たとえば「利用者の環境適応を考慮した暑熱環境対策」[http://www.kinki-shasej.org/upload/pdf/20170922.No328.2.pdf] など)。ちょっと暑くても快適だと感じられたり、心地よい場所を探して動いたり、ということですが、半屋外環境は人間の能動性を促す環境といえます。そんな場所であれば、気軽なコミュニケーションも期待できそうです。

I have introduced some examples of the incorporation of ecological cycles into architectural practice, using such natural elements as snow, ground heat, solar energy, and the wind. Their use leads to the emergence of distinctive structural characteristics in each building. One such characteristic worth noting in all these designs is the appearance of intermediate areas that function as thermal environments incorporating and utilizing these cyclical natural elements.

Practice	Cyclical Element	Incorporating Area	Incorporation Method	Effect
Villa in Hakuba	Snow, ground heat	Roofed plaza	"Wardrobe" change	Ebb and flow of ground surface
Omukai-san	Solar energy	Dayroom	Grouped roofs	Warm yet open to the outdoors
House in Fukasawa	Wind	Atrium terrace	Green louvers	Cool breezes, edible plants

Because they are both stimulating and comfortable, these intermediate areas encourage interaction with the outside. In the Villa in Hakuba, for example, the roofed plaza is a milder environment than the actual outdoors, yet offers an always refreshing view of the surrounding woods. I wrote that the roofed plaza allows one to enjoy a sensation of ebb and flow in the ground surface. Whether the season is hot or cold, one is constantly aware of the outdoors, and new discoveries always await. In my plan, the bathtub occupies a small hut built atop the plaza, affording even more opportunities to commune with nature. In the Omukai-san facility, the dayrooms stay warm despite the ample use of glass that brings residents into close contact with the courtyard even while indoors. The intermediate area of the House in Fukasawa offers the added pleasure of raising plants.

These thermal-environment intermediate areas can be described as spaces that reflect ecological cycles. In so doing they remind us that we, too, coexist with nature. ★38

★38
Research by Junta Nakano, a professor at Tokai University, shows that in semi-outdoor environments where people must adapt to the environment, their range of thermal comfort becomes greater than in fully indoor environments (see, for example, "Mitigation of Hot Environment Considering Thermal Adaptation of Occupants" [https://www.kinki-shasej.org/upload/pdf/20170922.No328.2.pdf]). Even if it's a bit warm, for instance, people may still feel comfortable, or they may seek out a more comfortable spot. In this sense a semi-outdoor environment has the effect of stimulating human activity, which suggests that it may also stimulate casual communication among residents.

3　2つの循環・融合の意図

The Fusion of the Two Cycles

3-1　ヴェネチア・ビエンナーレでの違和感
Misgivings at the Venice Biennale

　建築を、建築内外の動的な関係性を調整する存在だと考えるとき、僕は、人的な往来や交流といった流れと、熱や風といった物理環境的な流れの、その両方に等しく興味があります。これまで設計してきた作品を改めて眺めてみると、それら2つの関心に基づく2つの作品群に分かれます。

　2016年に、第15回ヴェネチア・ビエンナーレ国際建築展における日本館展示に招待されました★39。日本館キュレーターは山名善之氏（東京理科大学教授）で、「en［縁］」というテーマが掲げられました。繋がり、関係という意味での「縁」を、建築の実践とともに、世界に紹介しようという意図です。人、モノ、地域という3種類の関係性に分けて、12組の建築家が手がけた建築やその状況が展示されました。吉阪隆正設計の日本館の空間構成を巧みに利用した展示計画（会場構成はteco）もあいまって日本館の展示は評判を呼び、審査員特別表彰を受けるなど盛況でした★40。僕は《食堂付きアパート》を展示し、地域資源との関係のなかで、住むことと働くこととが融合した生活環境の可能性を提示しました。ここで僕は建築単体を取り出して見せることはせず、周囲の都市空間のでき方とともに建築を展示したのですが、建築と都市の連続性について、多くの観客の興味・関心を集めました★41。僕にとってこの展示の経験は貴重で、改めて「縁」という言葉と向き合ったのですが、「縁」という言葉は、人と環境の双方の関係性を含んだ言葉なのではないか、と理解するに至りました。つまり、もともとの僕の興味と重なるテーマを、日本館は掲げていたように思います。

If we think of architecture as something that adjusts the dynamic relations between a structure's interior and exterior, I would say that I am interested in the flow of human movements and interactions, but equally interested in the flow of environmental phenomena like heat and wind. Taking a fresh look at the works I have designed so far, I think they can be divided into two groups according to those two interests.

In 2016 we were invited to exhibit in the Japan Pavilion at the 15th International Architecture Exhibition, La Biennale di Venezia. ★39 The pavilion's curator, Professor Yoshiyuki Yamana of the Tokyo University of Science, proposed a theme of *en* (縁), meaning "relations" or "connections." His idea was to introduce this concept to the world along with examples of its practice in architecture. The exhibition featured works by architects from 12 offices, categorized into three types of connection: among people, things, and localities.

The exhibition (designed by teco), which made skillful use of the pavilion designed by Takamasa Yoshizaka, was very favorably received, even winning a Special Mention from the jury. ★40 I exhibited "Apartments with a Small Restaurant," highlighting the potential of living environments that blend work and home life while connecting with local resources. Instead of displaying only the building, I included the surrounding urban space in my exhibit. This concept of continuity between architecture and city attracted the interest of many visitors. ★41 The exhibition was a valuable experience that gave me an opportunity to contemplate the word *en* from a new perspective; I arrived at an understanding of *en* as embracing connections both among people and with their environment. In other words, the Japan Pavilion's theme resonated with my own personal interests.

When I viewed other exhibits from this standpoint, however, I experienced strong feelings of discomfort. Put bluntly, they displayed a partiality toward human connections, and my discomfort stemmed from their emphasis on the lively hustle and bustle engendered by human interaction. Without questioning their tacit assumptions about livelihoods and residences, they deftly wove scenarios in which people were half-coerced into interacting with one another. My thought was that these relationships would not be sustainable if they were not voluntary.

★39
イタリア・ヴェネチアで行われる国際展で、建築部門の展覧会は2年に一度行われます。ヴェネチア・ビエンナーレはもともと美術の国際展として1895年に始まり、建築部門の展覧会は1975年から不定期に、1980年になってビエンナーレ形式で開催されるようになりました。各国のパビリオンでの展示は国別対抗といった雰囲気もありますが、パビリオンそのものも各国の建築文化を反映していて、展示内容とともに見応えがあります。日本館は吉阪隆正の設計による素晴らしい建築で、離散的で均整の取れた構造体による流動的な空間を特徴としています。

The architecture section of this international exposition in Venice, Italy takes place every two years. The Venice Biennale began as an international art exhibition in 1895, with the Architecture Exhibition added in 1975; initially held at irregular intervals, it became biennial in 1980. While the shows presented at each country's pavilion have something of the flavor of a contest among nations, the pavilions themselves reflect the architectural cultures of their respective countries and are worth looking at in their own right. The Japan Pavilion designed by Takamasa Yoshizaka is a marvelous work of architecture distinguished by the fluidity of the spaces formed by its discrete, symmetrical structures.

★40
会期中の日本館入場者数は16万人を超えました（国際交流基金「平成28年度業務実績等報告書」）。

The number of visitors to the Japan Pavilion during the exhibition exceeded 160,000 (Japan Foundation, "2016 Detailed Annual Report on Business Results").

★41
専門家も多く来場しましたが、それと同じくらいヴェネチア市民がいたのが驚きでした。都市と建築の双方に関心があり、目の肥えた観客だと思いました。

Though professionals made up a large proportion of the visitors, what surprised me was that a comparable number were residents of Venice. My impression was that they were people with a discriminating eye and an interest in both architecture and urban planning.

このような観点でいろいろな展示を見ていると、大きな違和感を感じざるをえませんでした。端的にいえば、人的な関係性の偏重です。人と人の繋がり、それがもたらす賑わいが強調されることの違和感です。生活や住宅が暗黙のうちに前提としていることを問うことなしに、巧妙な物語が導入され、半ば強制的に人々が向き合わされている。そのことがまず、内発的でないがゆえに、持続的でない、と考えます。

人的関係性の偏重は環境問題への言及の少なさにも繋がっていて、とにかく地球上で、人間だけが浮かれているような滑稽さがありました。総合ディレクターを務めた建築家アレハンドロ・アラヴェナが掲げた全体テーマは「Reporting from the Front」。社会課題に対して建築には何ができるのか、各国が報告せよ、といったテーマです。各国が競うように「病気自慢」をしていたという構図がありますから、国際的な共通課題である気候変動問題が取り上げられにくいのは致し方ないかもしれません。しかし、建築の評価が、人的関係性のためのカンフル剤としての評価に偏っている印象はけっして心地よいものではなく、刹那的な印象を受けました。

この出展がひとつのきっかけとなって、2017年には、Vitra Design Museum（ドイツ）での「Together! The New Architecture of the Collective」展に招待されました。世界各地のあたらしい考えに基づいた集合住宅が集められた展覧会です★42。会場はフランク・O・ゲーリーがデザインしたギャラリーで、光栄にも、4作のみに与えられた詳細展示の機会を得ました。豪華なトップライトのある空間が展示の舞台でした。《食堂付きアパート》をヴェネチア・ビエンナーレとは別の観点で展示し、職住一体という形式の住宅には持続的なコミュニティをつくる可能性があること、どのようにして実現し現状はどうなっているのかというプロセス、この2点を提示しました。

ほかの作品と比べて改めて認識したのは、《食堂付きアパート》は半屋外空間が多いことです。立体路地と呼んでいるところはほぼすべて屋根付きの外部空間になっており、しかもそれが個々のSOHO住宅のすぐ外側にあることが、ほかの展示作品に比べて、形態的な特徴でした。そこは雨が降り込まず、風を取り込む場所であり、日々の生活や仕事の場所の延長として自然なかたちで使われています。身体的に心地よいから開く、そこから交流やら交換やらが始まる――社会的な観点からのみ建築をつくるのではなく、環境的な観点から交流の場所をデザインすることの重要性を再認識しました。

★42
ドイツ・ヴァイル・アム・ラインのVitra Design Museum（2017年6月～9月）、ベルギー・グラン・オルニュのCID Centre for Innovation and Design at the Grand Hornu（2018年3月～6月）、ドイツ・ライプツィヒのGrassi Museum（2018年11月～2019年3月）、スイス・ジュネーヴのMaison de l'Architecture（2019年5月～6月）の4カ所を巡回するほどの盛況ぶりです。キュレーターはヨーロッパ都市部の人口流入による住宅難を背景にしたあたらしい住宅への関心の高まりを示していると考えています。なお、Vitra Design Museumでの展示には、28,000人あまりが訪れたと聞きます。

This is a major exhibition that has travelled to four venues: the Vitra Design Museum in Weil am Rhein, Germany (June–September 2017), the CID - Centre for Innovation and Design at Grand Hornu, Belgium (March–June 2018), the Grassi Museum in Leipzig, Germany (November 2018–March 2019), and the Maison de l'Architecture in Geneva, Switzerland (May–June 2019). The curators viewed the show's success as indicative of a growing interest in new housing concepts against a backdrop of housing shortages due to the population inflow into European cities. I was told that over 28,000 people visited the exhibition at the Vitra Design Museum.

This bias in favor of human connections could also be seen in a dearth of references to environmental problems; in any event it seemed predicated on the absurd notion that the earth is populated only by human beings. The overall theme announced by architect Alejandro Aravena, the general director of the exhibition, was "Reporting from the Front." The idea was to encourage reports from each country on how architecture might respond to social issues. Since the framework was a sort of competition among countries over "who is the sickest," it is perhaps inevitable that it could not readily accommodate issues like climate change that are shared by all countries. Even so, I could not avoid the discomfiting impression that these evaluations of architectural works leaned excessively toward evaluations of their efficacy as stimulants of human connectivity, an effect that would be transient at best.

One opportunity resulting from my exhibit at the Biennale was an invitation to participate in the exhibition *Together! The New Architecture of the Collective* at the Vitra Design Museum in Germany in 2017. This show featured designs for collective housing based on new concepts at sites around the world. ★42 Held in a gallery designed by Frank O. Gehry, the exhibition provided space for detailed exhibits of only four works, of which I was honored to submit one. For my exhibit, which appeared in a space lit by a glorious skylight, I chose to introduce "Apartments with a Small Restaurant" from a different perspective than I had at the Venice Biennale, focusing on two aspects: the potential for creating sustainable communities with a live/work housing format, and the current status of the process of making this a reality.

When comparing my work with the others on exhibit, I was reminded again of the large number of semi-outdoor spaces in the "Apartments with a Small Restaurant." Among its distinguishing characteristics are the fact that nearly all of what I call the "cubic alley" consists of roofed outdoor space, and that it is located immediately outside the SOHO units. The alley is a place where rain does not enter, but the wind does, making it amenable to use as a natural extension of spaces for day-to-day life or work. Once more I was made aware of the possibilities of designing places for interaction not only from a societal perspective but also from an environmental one. Because they are physically comfortable, such places encourage people to open their doors, leading to interactions and exchanges of various sorts.

3–2　従来のコミュニティ論への違和感
Misgivings about Conventional Ideas of Community

　賑わい重視のコミュニティへの疑問はしかし、ヴェネチアでの展覧会に留まる話ではありません。むしろ、日本において常日頃抱いていた違和感です。

　「コミュニティする」という言葉を聞いたことがあります。そのときに感じた気持ち悪さを忘れることができません。コミュニティ＝イベント、という解釈になっているのです。

　イベントを打って人を集め、普段は出会わない人々が交流をする。素晴らしい話です。イベント自体に反対などしません。しかし、内発的でないものは継続できない。その理由から、賑わい重視のコミュニティ論には違和感を感じます。コミュニティ＝イベントという解釈は、おそらくかつての地域共同体に見られた祭りや儀礼への憧憬から始まっているのだと思いますが、そもそも祭りや儀礼はコミュニティが存在してこその事後的なものです。また、コミュニティの場のデザインについての話になると、たいてい、それは共用部のデザインの話になる。そこも違和感満載です。

　私的領域と公的領域のあいだに位置づけられる、自分たちの生活のために自分たちで決定できる空間と仕組みのことをコミュニティと呼びたいと思います。そのとき、あってもなくてもいいもの、無理矢理付け加えるもの、コミュニティはそんな「トッピング」のようなものではないはずです。子育て、教育、介護、防犯に関わる生活支援は特に、物理的に近いこと、身体的・直接的であることが重要な意味を持ちます。このような生活の手段としてのコミュニティは、場所とともに語らなくてはならない。コミュニティの場のデザインは、私的領域のデザインとともに語らなくてはいけない。そのように考えます★43。

　話はすこし逸れますが、2-2で取り上げた《上総喜望の郷おむかいさん》を設計していたときに、福祉法人の理事長である樋口さんから教わったことがあります。それは、知的障害者の住宅は国の補助金によって誘導されているが、立地条件を鑑みていない、ということでした。

　これまでは人里離れた場所に大規模施設として入所施設（それもかつては更正施設という名称でした）がつくられていましたが、徐々に、街中に立地するグループホームに移行しています。外観上は一軒家のような大きさです。この変化の背景にあるのは、障害者も健常者も地域社会で一緒に暮らす、という理念です。しかしながら、近隣とトラブルにならないように、施設設置者と設計者が「配慮」として、頑丈な境界や厳重なドアを設け、結果として知的障害者の方々が汲々と暮らしているケースがあるのも事実だ、と★44。

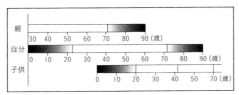

人生のなかで他人に頼る時期
Dependency on others during an individual's lifetime.

My discomfort with notions of community that prioritize liveliness and prosperity was not limited to the exhibitions at the Venice Biennale; actually it was something I had felt in Japan for some time.

There is a Japanese catchphrase, *community suru*, literally "making" or "doing" community. I will never forget the queasy feeling that came over me when I first heard that term, phrased as if community were a kind of event.

Hold an event, bring people together, get people who might otherwise never meet to interact. It's a wonderful thought. I have nothing against events per se. However, if they are not spontaneous and voluntary, they will not last. That is my objection to the keep-it-lively concept of community. The perception of community as event stems, I think, from a yearning for the festivals and rituals that once flourished in rural communities in Japan. But those events occurred precisely because a community existed, not the other way around. Moreover, discussions of "community design" almost inevitably turn out to be about designs for common-use spaces. That, too, gives me pause.

I would like to use the word "community" to refer to a space and framework, positioned between the private and public realms, that people can define as they wish in order to enhance their own lives. A community in this case is not supposed to be some sort of "icing on the cake" that is unnecessary yet is imposed on people without their say in the matter. It is particularly important that livelihood support related to child rearing, education, caregiving, and crime prevention be directly person-to-person and in close physical proximity. We must discuss "community" as a means of livelihood support in the same context as "place." And we must discuss the design of community space in the same context as the design of private space. This is what I believe. [43]

Allow me to digress a bit. When I was designing the Omukai-san facility introduced in Section 2-2, I learned from Atsuo Higuchi, chief director of the social welfare corporation Mizuki-kai, that residential facilities for intellectually disabled people are promoted by subsidies from the national government, but that these do not take local conditions into account.

Until recently, large-scale residential facilities (which were once known as rehabilitation facilities) were built in secluded locations, but the trend has gradually shifted toward group homes, built in urban areas, that look like ordinary houses. Behind this shift is the idea that disabled and non-disabled people should live together in the same community. However, there are cases where facility proprietors and designers take "precautions" against trouble with the neighbors by erecting robust boundaries, strictly guarded doors and so on, with the result that the intellectually disabled residents live in a state of constraint. [44]

★43
東京大学教授で建築計画学者である大月敏雄氏は、人生のなかで他人に頼る度合いをグラフ（左図）にしながら、自立的と思える期間はせいぜい10年と述べています（たとえば、『住まいと町とコミュニティ』王国社、2017、p.15）。人生90年としても、残りの80年は地域空間やそこに住む人々に支えられながら生きていくことが必要な時期であるとし、非空間型の地縁の可能性を認めながらも、空間型地縁の重要性について具体的に述べています。
University of Tokyo professor and architectural planner Toshio Otsuki has plotted the degree of dependence on others over the course of an individual's lifetime and finds that people experience at most 10 years of independence (see, for example, *Sumai to machi to community* [Home, Town, and Community], Okokusha, 2017, p. 15). He states that out of a 90-year lifespan, the remaining 80 years require support from one's local environment or people living there, and makes explicit the importance of spatial communities, even while recognizing the possibilities of non-spatial communities as well.

★44
建築家もその「配慮」の具現化に荷担していることに自覚的でありたいと思います。
I would like architects to acknowledge their complicity in giving form to such "precautions."

一方で樋口さんらは、入所施設でありながら、小舎制をいち早く採り入れてきました。20年以上前につくった最初の施設（1995年供用開始）に今でも見学者が訪れると聞きます。そして、《上総喜望の郷おむかいさん》では小舎制をさらに進め、5〜6人というグループホームと同じ規模感の住宅として、入所施設のあたらしい姿を実現しました。敷地にゆとりがあり、フェンスを張り巡らせる必要もなく、集落へと繋がる道路側のみ生け垣で軽く、優しく、仕切られているだけです。建築の工夫として内外が連続していること、いろいろな小さな居場所を分散させていることも相まって、自分が過ごす場所を自分で選べ、ゆったりとした生活を過ごせていると聞きます。

　ほかにも、樋口さんたちと「何をつくるか」からじっくり話し合ってきたので、かつての入所施設と《上総喜望の郷おむかいさん》とは、同じ入所施設でも大きく異なります。大切なことは、「場所」と「生活」は切り離せない、ということです。グループホームという形式だけが目的となり、どんな場所で、どのような空間をつくり、どのような生活を営むかが不問にされていることは、生活の場としてあってはならない。非・場所のシステムは危険である。僕はこのプロジェクトを通して、「場所」とセットになった住宅を設計しなくてはいけない、ということを学んだわけです★45。

　そしてこのことは、トッピング的な非・場所的コミュニティ論に対する違和感を決定的にした経験でした。

　一時期、「アクティビティを見せる」として、ガラス張りの建築が流行りました。写真映えを優先させた結果の居心地の悪さから、すぐにカーテンで閉じられ、段ボールが貼られ、アクティビティは見えなくなるものです。これもまた、賑わい重視、視覚偏重の悪弊のひとつだと思います。

★45
福祉発のコミュニティ論がしばしば、非・場所、アンチ・空間になるのはなぜだろうか。ながらく抱いている疑問です。
以前、福祉問題で著名な方が講演で「目の前の人を全身でケアしようとするのであれば、廊下が狭いからできない、浴室が古いから対応できないなど、空間や建築のせいにしてケアを怠ることは許されない」と述べていました。そのような、ケアに対する責任感からなのでしょうか。

Mr. Higuchi and his associates were, in fact, among the earliest developers of cottage-style residential facilities in Japan. Their first facility, built over two decades ago (it opened in 1995), is still visited by observers today, I am told. With Omukai-san they took the cottage system even further, creating a new form of residential facility with cottages housing five or six people, the same scale as a group home. Thanks to the spacious lot there is no need for an encircling fence; the only indication of a boundary is an attractive, unimposing hedge facing the road that leads to the village. Designed as it is to bring interior and exterior into proximity in a dispersed layout of many small "places to be," the structure has, I'm told, made it possible for residents to enjoy a relaxing daily life during which they can choose where they would like to spend their time.

Additionally, our thorough discussions with Mr. Higuchi et al. about what sort of place this should be ensured that Omukai-san would be quite unlike other residential facilities. The most important point of these discussions was that "place" and "life" are inextricably linked. If one is only concerned with the superficial format of a group home—without giving any thought to what sort of space to create in what sort of place, and what sort of life residents will live there—then the facility cannot possibly function successfully as a place to live. The risk of creating a "non-place" is high. Thanks to this project, I learned that housing must always be designed with "place" in mind. ★45

The experience was also decisive in solidifying my misgivings about superficial, "non-place" concepts of community.

Once upon a time, glass-covered buildings that showed off the activities going on inside were in fashion. Prioritizing photogenicity in this way, however, produced uncomfortable spaces that the inhabitants sought to remedy by covering the windows with cardboard, shutting the curtains, and otherwise hiding their activities from view. That, I believe, is another example of the pernicious consequences of an overemphasis on liveliness and visibility.

★45
Something I have long puzzled over is why the notions of community that emerge from the welfare-care field so often result in non-places or anti-spaces.

Some time ago, someone well known for their views on welfare issues said, "If you intend to give your all to caring for the person before you, then there is no excuse for neglecting that care and blaming the space or the building—complaining, for example, that the corridor is too narrow or the bathroom is too old." Perhaps the problem lies with this attitude of expecting nothing from structures or spaces.

3–3　融合の可能性を感じたきっかけ

Realizing Possibilities for Fusion

　「Socialな循環」と「Ecologicalな循環」。これら2つの循環のうち、人的な関係性の循環が偏重されている違和感をここまで書いてきたわけですが、そこに環境的な循環を重ね合わせて建築をつくろうと思いついたことについて、述べようと思います。

　2つの循環を重ねるとはどういうことか。参考になる体験を紹介します。

　小学生のときに僕は、東京の下町、門前仲町の団地に住んでいました。なかなか面白い環境で、団地全体が「学童保育施設」のような有り様でした。300戸くらいの団地ですが、あちこちの住宅でいろいろな習い事教室が開かれていました。絵画教室、ピアノ教室、英語教室、本の読み聞かせ、天体観測。廊下も遊び場だった子どもたちにとって、いろいろな教室が「ブラウジング」できたわけです。先生はそれぞれの住宅の、おもにお母さんだったのですが、人となりがわかる開放感と顔の見える安心感から、団地の外の人も通ってきていました。

　習い事教室が団地内のあちこちで開かれていた理由を考えてみると……。

　まず人的資源の存在は前提です。当時は（今もかもしれませんが）国家公務員の家族が住むための団地で、大学卒で専門的な知識を持つ母親が比較的多かったのだと思います。

　また、職住が近接している下町の地域性も影響していたでしょう。小学校のまわりには、商店街や築地に勤める人たちの住む界隈がそれぞれありました。お寺の息子もいました。子ども心にも、家業が明らかで、地域社会を育てる人たちの存在が見えるわかりやすさがありました。

Social cycles and ecological cycles: of the two, I have been talking about my discomfort with excessive partiality to the former, i.e., cycles of human relations. Here I would like to discuss some ideas that have occurred to me about creating architecture that overlays ecological and social cycles.

What does it mean to overlay these two types of cycle? Let me use a personal experience to explain.

When I was in elementary school I lived in an apartment complex in Monzen-Nakacho, an old downtown Tokyo neighborhood. It was a rather interesting environment, in which the entire complex functioned as a sort of after-school facility for elementary schoolkids. Among the approximately 300 apartments in the complex, several were open as learning spaces. There was an art class, a piano class, an English class, a book-reading class, an astronomy class. The resident children, for whom the apartment house corridors were play spaces, could go "browsing" from class to class. The teachers were mostly mothers living in these various apartments. They were friendly, safe environments that attracted users from outside the complex as well.

Why did all these classrooms open up in an apartment complex?

The first reason is the presence of human resources. At the time, this complex was intended (perhaps it still is) to house the families of civil servants in the national government; therefore a relatively high proportion of the mothers were college graduates with professional experience.

Another influence, I believe, was the character of this district of Tokyo, where home and work were in close proximity. Near my elementary school were neighborhoods with concentrations of people working in the shopping district or at the Tsukiji Fish Market. Children of Buddhist temple priests also attended the school. It was easy to identify the roles people played in the community, so even kids knew about one another's family businesses.

住宅内の空間配列も特徴的でした。民間の集合住宅ほどいわゆるフロンテージセーブが徹底されていたわけではなく、間口がやや広めで奥行きが浅いという平面形状でした。内部は、多少のバリエーションはありましたが、基本的には共用廊下に台所が面し、玄関を開けるとダイニングキッチン、奥に行くと2寝室に分かれるという間取りでした。共用廊下側は壁だらけではありましたが、空間配列だけ取り出せば、《食堂付きアパート》に近いといえなくもありません。そのダイニングキッチンが、習い事教室の場所でした。

しかしこれらだけでは、習い事教室が団地のあちこちで行われ、興味深くブラウジングできた現象を説明できません。習い事教室をしている住宅以外も含めて、あちこちの住宅で鉄の玄関扉が開け放たれていたことを思い出します。それは単に、扉を開けると風が抜けて心地よかったからです。

この団地は、隅田川のほとりにあります。大川と呼ばれた隅田川は文字通り大きな川であり、風の通り道でした★46。エアコンが今ほど普及していなかったこともありますが、風が豊かな敷地で、奥行きが比較的浅いという平面形状から、玄関扉とベランダの掃き出しのサッシを開放すると、風がよく抜けて、涼しかったことを覚えています。心地いいから扉を開けていて、それゆえに、習い事教室の様子が廊下に伝わっていました。共用廊下とそこに面した開口部の使い方について、共通認識のようなものができあがっていました。ここは、いってみれば、コミュニティを体現する空間です。

都市規模の風の循環のなかに建築が置かれている。心地よいから開く。そこに人的な関係性が重ねられる。その結果、団地のなかに、小商いの空間が連なって出現していたのだといえます。小商いの空間群は、持続的です。個々人に内在しているスキルを発揮する空間ですので。

★46
スパコンを使ったシミュレーション例（盛夏の14:00）。隅田川からの風が団地に導入されていることがわかります。近年は、大規模河川近傍の建物に対して形態制限をすることで、内陸部まで海風を導入することが検討されています。

In this simulation done on a supercomputer for 2 p.m. in midsummer, it is clear that the wind from the Sumida River is drawn into the housing complex. In recent years there have been studies on drawing sea breezes inland by imposing structural restrictions on buildings along major rivers.

スパコンを使ったシミュレーション例（部分）
Supercomputer simulation (partial image).

The spatial configuration of each apartment unit was also distinctive. The "frontage-saving" (narrow entrance) format was not taken to the extreme seen in privately-owned apartment houses, so units were laid out with relatively wide frontage and shallow depth. Though there was some variation in the interior layouts, most units had the kitchen facing the common passageway, so the entrance opened into a dining-kitchen area, with two bedrooms in the rear. Though the side facing the common passageway was almost entirely solid wall, in other respects the spatial arrangement was remarkably similar to that of the Apartments with a Small Restaurant. These dining-kitchens served as the classroom spaces in the apartments.

However, these factors alone do not explain the phenomenon of classrooms scattered throughout the complex that lent themselves to serious browsing. I recall that many people left the steel front doors of their apartments open, and not only those serving as classrooms. The simple reason is that opening the door allowed a pleasant flow of fresh air through the apartment.

This apartment complex is on the bank of the Sumida River. It is a wide waterway (it was once known as *O-kawa*, the Big River) that serves as a conduit for the wind. ★46 In those days air conditioning was not as common as now, but the site was a breezy one and our apartment was relatively shallow and wide, so I remember how cool it felt when we opened the front door and the dust-outlet window onto the veranda in back to let the wind blow through. People opened their doors because it felt more comfortable, but it also had the effect of transmitting the ambience of the classrooms to the passageway outside. Thus the way people used the common passageways and the apertures facing them fostered something like a mutual awareness of what we might call a community space.

Buildings are located in the midst of a cycle of wind circulating through a city. Residents open their doors because the wind feels good, which enhances human connections, which leads to the emergence of an aggregate of small-business spaces throughout an apartment complex. These small-business spaces are sustainable because they manifest skills inherent in individual residents.

4　建築を 2 つの循環のなかに位置づける
Positioning Architecture within Two Cycles

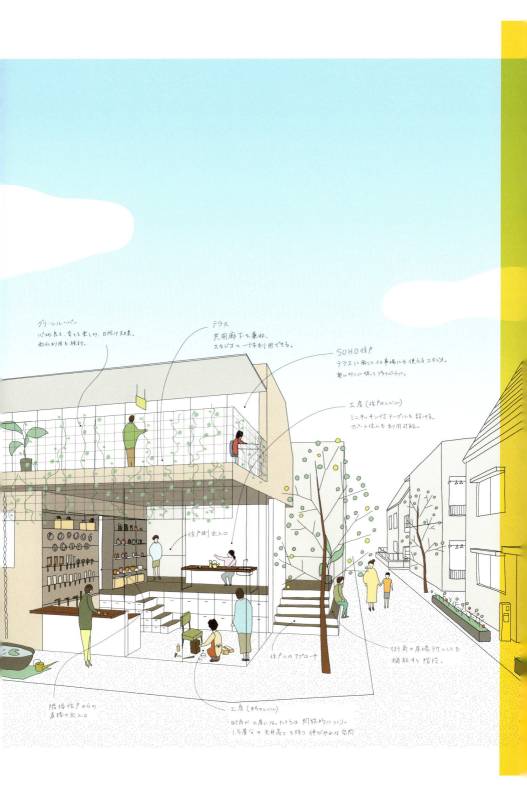

4-1　2つの循環を重ねる──《五本木の集合住宅》
Overlaying Two Cycles: Gohongi Housing

4　建築を2つの循環のなかに位置づける　124

ここで今までの話を整理しておこうと思います。

　「Socialな循環」とは、地域における人と人の関係が連鎖していく様を指しています。各所に林立する小さな公共的な空間が、人と人との小さな交換やそれに伴う交流を支えます。大きな視野に立てば、局所的な交換・交流が連鎖していき、人と人の関係は地域のなかで循環します。情けは人のためならず、の世界観です。その空間は何も「公共施設」として準備される必要はなく、住宅の「中の」外向きの場所としてつくられることも十分に可能です。僕たちはそれが私的領域における中間領域として設けられることを提唱し、これまで実践を続けてきました。

　この中間領域が私的領域のなかに設けられる、というところが重要で、ここでの中間領域は交換の場です。〈小さな経済〉、つまり、仕事場であったり、お店であったり、趣味や特技を展開する小商いの場所であったり、そういった交換の場です。住人の内発的な活動の場であるがために、持続的・継続的な場として外部に開かれ続けます。

　では、「Socialな循環」の舞台である中間領域はどのようにつくられ、どのように維持されたらいいのか。どんな空間であれば、人的な関係性が円滑に、自然に、持続するのだろうか。そのような問いから、「Ecologicalな循環」に着目することを考えました。

　「Ecologicalな循環」とは、自然エネルギーや自然資源の地球規模・都市規模の循環を指しています。太陽光、太陽熱、雨、雪、風、地熱、など。環境的な流れをどのように建築に取り入れ、あるいは排除し、空間の快適さをつくりだすかの手法は、建築の長い歴史のなかでさまざまに発達してきました。

　人的な交流の中間領域を、Ecologicalな循環で支える。無理をしない方法でつくられた快適さは、ナチュラルな交流を促すのではないか。そんな予感から、2つの循環のなかに、建築を位置づけてみようと思い立ったわけです。

　建築を、内部空間と外部空間を区画する技術だと位置づければ、これら2つの循環は、それぞれ、人と自然という大きな要素を扱うものです。その意味では、2つの循環という観点から建築をつくろうとすることは、本質的な作業であるように考えます。

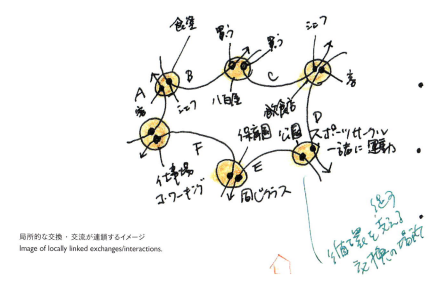

局所的な交換・交流が連鎖するイメージ
Image of locally linked exchanges/interactions.

Here I would like to summarize my discussion so far.

A social cycle is a state in which relations among people in a locality are linked together. An aggregate of small public spaces in various locations supports small exchanges among individuals and the interactions that accompany them. Looking at the big picture, these localized exchanges and interactions are connected in a way that allows interpersonal relations to circulate through the community, in the sense that "what goes around comes around." There is no need to prepare special public facilities to provide such spaces, and it is entirely feasible to create them by providing outward-oriented spaces within residences. We have proposed, and put into practice, the creation of such spaces in the form of intermediate areas that are a part of private areas.

It is crucial that such intermediate areas be located within private space as places of exchange—in other words, as "small economies": workplaces, shops, small businesses that showcase personal hobbies or skills. Because these are places of spontaneous activity by residents, they have sustainability and continuity as spaces open to the outside.

How, then, do we create, and maintain, the intermediate areas that set the stage for this social cycle? What sort of space facilitates smooth, natural, and sustainable human relations? It was the effort to answer this question that prompted me to think about ecological cycles.

An ecological cycle refers to the circulation of natural energy or resources, whether on a global or citywide scale. Sunlight, solar heat, rain, snow, wind, and geothermal heat are examples. Over the long history of architecture, many methods have been developed for incorporating the flow of environmental elements into buildings, or removing them from buildings, in order to make living and working spaces more comfortable.

We use natural energy to sustain intermediate areas for human interaction. My instinct is that comfort achieved through stress-free means facilitates natural interactions. That is the impetus for my interest in positioning architecture amid these two cycles.

If architecture is a technique for dividing space into an interior and an exterior, then these two cycles represent the utilization of the major elements of people and nature respectively in creating those spaces. In that sense, designing structures with these two cycles in mind is an essential part of architectural practice.

《五本木の集合住宅》は、仕事場兼用住宅が3戸集まってできた集合住宅です。各住宅のなかに、仕事場があります。「Ecologicalな循環」として、雨水の循環に取り組みました。雨水を利用して涼しい風をつくりだし、それを取り込もうとするから仕事場を開く、そんな状況を想像しながらつくった集合住宅です。

　右の写真は夕立で建物が冷やされる様子を示す写真です。猛烈な風雨にたたきつけられて、下屋や外壁の表面温度はみるみるうちに下がり、濡れていない軒下に比べて7℃低い様子がわかります。夕立が降るまでは外壁や屋根はカンカンに熱かったから、温度低下は相当なはずです★47。こうしたことをつねづね体験していたので、雨を使おうと思ったのだと思います。

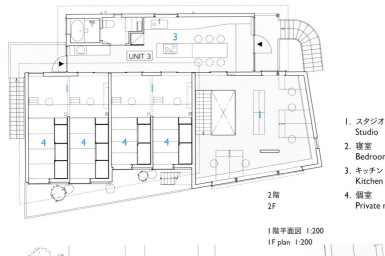

1. スタジオ Studio
2. 寝室 Bedroom
3. キッチン Kitchen
4. 個室 Private room

2階
2F

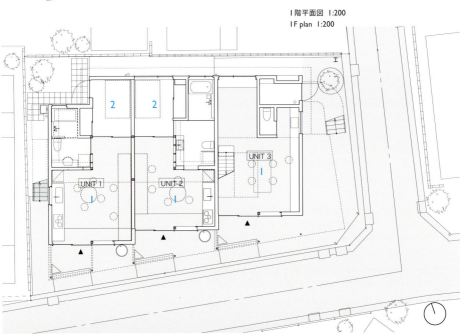

1階平面図 1:200
1F plan 1:200

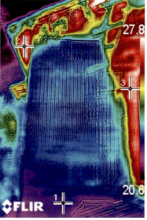

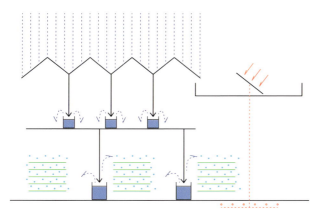

Ecologicalな循環のダイアグラム：雨水や太陽熱を使う形が屋根の形となって現れる
Ecological cycle diagram: The use of rainwater and solar heat determines the design of the roof.

★47
独立当初はこの古い木造家屋が事務所でした。夏場は暑くて暑くて仕事にならなかったので、夕立はむしろありがたかったものです。夕立がないと内壁や天井からの輻射熱で夜も暑かったことをよく覚えています。

This old wooden house was my office when I first went independent. In the summer it was so unbearably hot that I couldn't work, so I was always grateful for downpours. I remember that it was also hotter on rainless nights due to the radiant heat from the inner walls and ceiling.

"Gohongi Housing" is a multi-unit building comprising three live/work units. Each residence contains a workspace. I incorporated the circulation of rainwater as an ecological cycle, designing the apartments with the idea of opening up the workplace to import cooling breezes generated by the use of rainwater.

The photographs above show the cooling effect of a sudden shower on a building. After being pelted by an intense rainstorm, the surface temperature of the lean-to roof and the outer wall plunged to around 7℃ below that of the dry space under the eaves. Considering that the walls and roof were scorching hot before the rain came, that is a substantial decrease. ★47
I think I got the idea of utilizing rainfall from personally experiencing this phenomenon countless times.

　長屋形式で、それぞれの住宅は1階に入口があり、前面道路から直接入ります。ここでも《食堂付きアパート》と同様に、スタジオアクセスの形式を採りました。つまり、仕事場であるスタジオは玄関に付随して設けられ、奥に行くにつれてプライバシーの高い個室や水まわりが配置されている、という形式です。

　UNIT1、2は、1階で完結する住宅です。《食堂付きアパート》で紹介したようなフラット型のスタジオアクセスの形式です。UNIT3は僕の自宅兼事務所ですが、メゾネットとなっていて、2層吹き抜けの仕事場の奥に住宅部分が配置されています。

The units were laid out like row houses, with each residence having its entrance on the ground floor, accessible directly from the street. Here, too, I adopted a studio-access format as in the Apartments with a Small Restaurant, with the "studio" workspace just inside the entrance, and the bedroom, wet area and so on in the back.

Units 1 and 2 are residences fully contained on the ground floor, with studio access flush with the ground as in the case of the Apartments with a Small Restaurant. Unit 3 is my own residence-plus-office and is in a maisonette format, with a two-story studio perforated by an atrium, and my living quarters in the back.

《食堂付きアパート》と比べて、仕事場であるスタジオまわりのプランニングで工夫したことがあります。
　UNIT1、2は、サニタリー（トイレ、脱衣、浴室）を仕事場と個室の中間領域と位置づけました。《食堂付きアパート》を設計しているときに、各SOHO住宅内のトイレの扉の位置について悩んだのですが、その時は個室側から入るようにして、仕事場に来るお客さんやスタッフには食堂とシェアオフィスの共同トイレを使ってもらうかたちで整理しました★48。
　ところが、《五本木の集合住宅》の場合は、食堂にあたるような共用的な空間がありません。そこで、仕事場からも個室からも入れるような、ダブルアクセスのサニタリーとしました。その結果、大きめのサニタリーになりました。
　じつはひょんなことから、UNIT1、2の賃貸住宅には僕の両親が店子として入居することになり、2つの住宅を一体化して使っています。父親はいまだに自宅で仕事をしていますが、〈小さな経済〉の想定は若い住人像だったので、初めは戸惑いました。しかしながら、広いサニタリーで、かつ、そのアクセスが2方向からあることを考えると、将来、父親が仮に車椅子生活になっても、また、介護サービスが住宅内に入ってきても、円滑に暮らしていけそうです。つまり、住宅のなかに他者が入り込むことを前提にした住宅——スタジオアクセス形式に限らないと思いますが——は、若者であっても高齢者であっても、汎用性があることに気がつきました。

Compared to the Apartments with a Small Restaurant, some special planning went into the area around the studio-workplaces.

In Units 1 and 2, I positioned the sanitary area (toilet, changing area, bath) as an intermediate area between the studio and the bedroom. When I designed the Apartments with a Small Restaurant, I had a difficult time deciding where to place the door to the toilet in the SOHO units, finally making it accessible from the bedroom, so as to encourage staff and visitors in the studios to instead use the common toilet for the restaurant and shared office. ★48

However, the Gohongi Housing has no shared space equivalent to the other project's restaurant. I therefore designed the sanitary area with double access, from both the studio and the bedroom, and made it slightly larger.

In an unexpected development, my parents became tenants of Units 1 and 2, which they are using as a single unit. My father still works at home, but since I envisioned younger residents in my "small economy" design, I was concerned at first whether this arrangement would work. However, it turns out that the large sanitary area, with its access from two directions, will make it easy for my parents to continue living there even if my father should eventually require a wheelchair or in-home care. I realized that a residence designed on the premise of visits from non-family members—whether in studio-access or some other format—offers versatility to its residents, young or old.

★48
このあたりの詳細は、浅子佳英氏の司会で行われた、建築家の金野千恵氏との対談「施設から住まいへ――半パブリック空間のトイレ考」(LIXILビジネス情報サイト「パブリック・トイレのゆくえ」[https://www.biz-lixil.com/column/architecture_urban/public_toilet/dialogue_06/])で詳しく述べています。立体路地の地下の終点にある共用トイレの存在を前提とすることで、《食堂付きアパート》のSOHO住人は、地下から3階までをひとつの生活環境として捉えることが可能になっています。

For more details, see my dialogue with architect Chie Konno (moderated by Yoshihide Asako), "From Facilities to Residences: The Toilet in Semi-Public Spaces" (from the series *The Future of Public Toilets* on the LIXIL Business Information site [https://www.biz-lixil.com/column/architecture_urban/public_toilet/dialogue_06/]). The presence of a shared toilet at the basement end of the cubic alley encourages SOHO unit residents in the Apartments with a Small Restaurant to think of the entire space, from the basement to the third floor, as part of the same living environment.

UNIT3の工夫は、キッチンを仕事場と住宅の中間領域と位置づけたことです。仕事場と4つの個室とを並べ、これらを横断する廊下状空間をキッチンに割り当てました。建具の調整により、日中はキッチンは仕事場と一体の空間として使うことができ、コーヒーを淹れたり、賄いを食べたり、アットホームな打ち合わせ場所として使ったりしています。夜になると事務所側の引き戸を閉めることでキッチンは個室と一体となります。

　日中、スタッフが気兼ねなく使えるように、キッチン廊下は街路のような設えにしました。両端をガラス戸にして開放的にしたり（両端に外階段があるので実際に通り抜けられる）、外壁を入り込ませたり、各個室を仕切る引き戸は格子戸にしていたり、照明の色温度を下げすぎないようにしたり、などです。

　4つの個室は家族それぞれが使いますが、キッチン廊下を街路と見立て、各個室を住宅と見立て、手前に仕事場、奥に寝室、そのあいだはカーテンで仕切る、という構成にしています。子どもの仕事場は勉強部屋、親の仕事場は家事スペースや書斎として使われています。住宅のなかに小さな住宅が反復されているようなかたちです★49。

Unit 3 is characterized by the positioning of the kitchen as an intermediate area between the work and living spaces. The studio and four private rooms are laid out in a row, with the kitchen serving as a corridor-like space alongside them. Adjustment of the fittings allows the kitchen to be used during the day as an extension of the studio—a place to brew coffee, eat meals, or hold meetings in an at-home ambience. At night the sliding doors to the studio can be shut, unifying the kitchen with the four private rooms instead.

To encourage the staff to use the kitchen without hesitation during the day, I laid the kitchen corridor out like a street. Glass doors at each end (both leading to outdoor stairways) provide a feeling of openness, an exterior wall passes through the interior, sliding lattice doors are used to screen off the private rooms, and the color temperature of the lighting is not too low.

Each private room is used by a different member of my family. With the kitchen corridor serving as the street, each room is designed like a small residence, with a workplace in the front, a bedroom in the back, and a curtain between them. The children can use their workplace as a study, and the parents can use theirs as a study or a place to take care of household matters. It's like a row of small houses inside the larger house. ★49

★49

ほかにも、キッチン廊下が2つの外階段によって地上と繋がっていることも工夫した点です。子育てが終わったあとに、子どもが使っていた個室を他人に貸すことなどを考えて、このようにしました。

Another strategy was to link the kitchen corridor to the ground level via the outdoor stairways at each end. I did this with the thought that when our child-rearing days are over, we can rent out the rooms formerly used by the children.

さて、次に「Ecologicalな循環」をどう扱ったかについての話をしましょう。

住宅と街路との距離感をどのようにするか考えた結果、軒下を設け、その先端に視線を柔らかく遮るルーバーを、2mの高さまで設けました。また、仕事場は気積の大きな空間にしました。特に接地階で完結するUNIT1、2は、夜間にブラインドを下ろしていても高窓から風を取り込みたいと考えたためです。これらの断面操作は《食堂付きアパート》と異なる部分です。目の前が街路という接地階住宅であることを意識した結果です。

道路に面した1階に、3カ所、仕事場が現れるわけです。「Socialな循環」の種となる空間です★50。ここに重ねる「Ecologicalな循環」として、雨水という自然の資源の循環を選びました。雨水を使って軒下にクールスポットをつくりだすことができたら、仕事場であるスタジオに涼しい風を取り入れようと窓を開けるだろう。スタジオが身体的・精神的に心地よければ、仕事やコミュニケーションの質もまた豊かになるのではないか。そんなことを考えながら設計を進めました。

まず雨水をどのように集めるかを考えました。日常的に雨水を使おうとすると、使う場所ごとに水がめがあるほうが便利です。その結果、2階のギザギザ屋根に辿り着きました。この屋根は個室の単位を示すと同時に、雨水を分配する装置になっています。細かく折られた屋根で雨水を分散させて、一人ひとりの天水桶に分配します。天水桶は2階のベランダと1階の軒下に配置しています。雨量と集水面積と天水桶の容量をバランスさせました★51。

★50
お客さんや宅配便配達の方々が出たり入ったりし、またスタッフが外で模型をつくったり、色を塗ったりしています。実物大のサンプルを確認していると、近所の親子連れが横で眺めていたり。「家を建てたいんだけど」と飛び込みで仕事の相談が来たこともあります。近所の小学生が「家の鍵が開いていないからここで待たせてほしい」とひょっこり訪ねて来たこともありましたし、「何屋さんですか」と近くに住む人が入ってきたこともあります。昼間に人の姿が見えるというのは、意外と新鮮なのかもしれません。「Socialな循環」は少しずつ生まれています。

Visitors and delivery people come and go; the staff may be outside building or painting architectural models. Neighborhood parents and kids look on while we examine full-sized samples. People have dropped by to consult with us about building a house. Schoolkids on the way home have even asked us to let them wait here because their own house is locked. People living nearby have walked in and asked what we sell. No doubt it is novel to see a human presence here in the middle of the day.

Little by little, our social cycle is being born.

Next I would like to explain how I made use of an ecological cycle. To establish a sense of distance between the residences and the street, I decided to create a space under the eaves, with two-meter-high louvers on the outer edge providing a soft barrier to the line of sight. I also made each workplace a large-volume space. In Units 1 and 2, this makes it possible to draw the breeze in through high windows even when the blinds are shut at night. These cross-sectional strategies, which differ from those of the Apartments with a Small Restaurant, derive from the fact that the Gohongi Housing consists of ground-floor units with the street directly in front of them.

Three workplaces appear on the ground floor facing the street, forming a space that bears the seeds of a social cycle. ★50 I selected the circulation of rainwater, a natural resource, as an ecological cycle to apply to this space. Using rainwater to turn the area under the eaves into a cool spot should encourage users of the workplace studios to open their windows to let in the cool air. And if the studios are physically and emotionally comfortable, that should have a positive impact on the quality of the work and communications carried out there. Such was the thinking that inspired my design.

First I thought about how to collect the rainwater. If one intends to use rainwater on a day-to-day basis, it's convenient to have a rain barrel located at each place of use. This led me to the idea of the zigzag roof over the second floor. Besides accenting each private room, this roof functions as a device for distributing rainwater. The zigzag configuration disperses and apportions the water to a separate pair of rain barrels for each unit: one on the second-floor veranda and one on the first-floor space under the eaves. I took great pains to determine the right balance between rainfall volume, catchment area, and barrel capacity. ★51

★51
天水桶の容量は60リットル弱あり、水やり2週間分に相当します。夏は水やりの頻度を上げるので1週間分。気象データを概観すると、だいたい2週間に一回は雨が降るので（夏季はもう少し降るので）、60リットルの大きさが妥当と判断しました。なお、屋外水栓に灌水パイプを繋いでいるので、時間がないときは水道水で水やりすることも可能です。

The barrels hold a bit less than 60 liters, the equivalent of about two weeks of watering, or one week in the summer when we water more frequently. Since it rains here an average of about once every two weeks (a little more often in the summer), we thought that 60 liters was a suitable volume. There are also watering pipes connected to outdoor taps, so when we are busy we can use tap water for watering.

次に雨水の利用方法を考えました。ここでは、《深沢の住宅》で実践していたルーバーへの打ち水効果をブラッシュアップすることにしました。もっと小型化して、素材も、ルーバーそのものが土であり植栽であるという状態を目指しました。植栽ルーバーの基盤材は固化培土という素材で、混合した樹脂の働きによって、培養土が崩れません。保水性の高い固化培土によって表面温度を下げ、植栽の蒸散作用も含めてクールスポットをつくりだせないか。植物が風にそよぐ様は、風の可視化ともいえます。大きなガラスの向こうにそれが見え、窓を開けると心地よい風が流れ込む。それは雨と、雨を利用するための形態が支えている――雨水によってこんな一連の効果を生み出せないかと思ったわけです。

結果、どうだったか。軒下は、盛夏の日中において、外壁面と比べて20℃近く、前面道路と比べて30℃近く、表面温度が低い状態であることが確認できました。視線制御だけであれば金属製ルーバーも考えられましたが、輻射熱が激しくて、ここまで涼しげな軒下にはならなかったでしょう。そのことを考えれば、まずまずの成果だと思います★52。

★52
酒井敏ほか「フラクタル日除け――樹木の形に学ぶ新発想のヒートアイランド対策」(http://www.gaia.h.kyoto-u.ac.jp/~fractal/pdf/hi3_2010.pdf)によれば、直射日光を受ける物体の表面温度にとって、その物体の大きさは重要なパラメータです(「〔物体周囲の〕熱境界層の厚さは、理論的には物体の大きさの平方根に比例する」)。つまり、樹木の葉は、「そのサイズが小さいために表面にできる熱境界層が薄く空気に対する熱伝導率が高く、太陽から受け取った熱量を速やかに大気に逃がすことができる」。これらは《五本木の集合住宅》ができてから知ったことですが、グリーンルーバーそのものが高温化しないためには、培土が一体化していることとともに、ルーバーを覆う植栽の葉が小さいことも重要だといえます。

According to Satoshi Sakai et al. in "Fractal Sunshades: New Heat-Island Countermeasures Derived from Tree Shapes" (http://www.gaia.h.kyoto-u.ac.jp/~fractal/pdf/hi3_2010.pdf), the size of a physical object is an important parameter of its surface temperature when it receives direct sunlight: "The thickness of the thermal boundary layer [on the object's periphery] is theoretically proportional to the square root of the size of the object." In other words, tree leaves, "being small in size, are able to rapidly release the heat they receive from the sun into the atmosphere due to the thinness of the thermal boundary layer formed on their surface and their high thermal conductivity to the air." Though I learned this after completing the Gohongi Housing, it suggests that the small size of the plant leaves covering the green louvers may be as important as the uniform soil coverage in preventing the louvers from heating up.

Next I thought about how to utilize the rainwater. I decided to fine-tune the effects of sprinkling water on the louvers that we employed in the House in Fukasawa. I tried to make the louvers as small as possible so that they consist mainly of soil and plants. The bed for the green louvers is made of stabilized soil, in which resin mixed with the soil prevents it from disintegrating. I thought that this would create a cool spot due to the lower surface temperature produced by the high water retention of this soil combined with the transpiration effect of the plants. The plants rustling in the breeze are also a visible manifestation of the wind, if you will. Viewing that scene through the large windows should prompt one to open the windows and let the pleasant breeze inside. All of this would be thanks to the rain and our way of utilizing it. Such was the chain of effects generated by rainwater as I imagined it.

So, what was the actual outcome? We were able to confirm that at midday in midsummer, the surface temperature under the eaves was nearly 20°C lower than that of the outer wall, and nearly 30°C lower than that of the street in front. If our only concern was to restrict visibility we could have used metal louvers, but with their radiant heat the space under the eaves surely would not have gotten this cool. In that regard, I thought our results were reasonably good. ★52

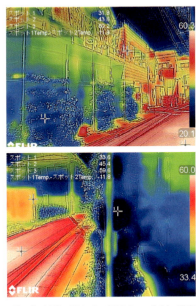

分散して集めた雨水の打ち水によって軒下にクールスポットをつくりだす
Cool spots formed under the eaves by sprinkling rainwater dispersed and collected in barrels.

ルーバーそのものを育てる楽しさもあります。固化培土にはポット苗と同じ大きさの穴を開けているので、ホームセンターで好きな苗を買ってきて簡単にインストールすることができます。今回は多年草ばかりだったので植え替えはないですが、それでも花や実がなるものを植えていると、道行く人々に声を掛けられます。重力に逆らってこんな植え方をして、というお叱りも受けつつ、ハーブをもらってよいかと声を掛けられることもありました。

天水桶は当初、ボウフラを心配しました。天水桶によって、メダカを入れたものとそうでないものをつくって実験しましたが、60リットルの天水桶であれば、雨によって適当に水が入れ替わるので、ボウフラはほとんど湧きませんでした。メダカがじゃんじゃん増殖して、近所の小学生の注目の的となっていました★53。

「Ecologicalな循環」として、雨水によるクールスポットを実現した結果、仕事場の外観は《食堂付きアパート》とはだいぶ様相の異なるものとなりました。フルハイトの窓ではなくて腰窓にして、一部採風用の小窓があります。窓際にデスクを置くなど居場所をつくれるようにして、窓辺の風景をつくろうとしたからです。

一番の違いは玄関の扉です。開き戸ではなくて引き違い戸にしています。グリーンルーバー越しの風を取り入れるために、風量を調整しやすい引き戸にしました。また引き戸は、雨が降っていても軒があれば風を取り入れることに向いています★54。

★53
簡単に紹介すると……。ボウフラを薬で防ぐことも考えましたが、それを植栽の水やりに使うことに抵抗があり、メダカや金魚がボウフラを食べることを利用しています。
天水桶の底に大磯砂を入れると、隙間にバクテリアが潜み、メダカのふんを分解してくれます。それを布袋草などの水草類が吸収し成長して葉陰が維持されると聞きました。メダカなどの小さな魚にとっては居心地のよい環境です。このように生態系をつくることでボウフラの発生を抑えようとしました。雨水を使っているだけに、pHも気になります。pH5を下回る酸性のときもありますが、コンクリ桝でつくった天水桶も、火鉢を転用した2階の水がめも、おそらくその素材ゆえに、数日〜2週間ほどすると弱アルカリ性に転んでいることがわかりました（右頁写真参照）。メダカは弱アルカリ性を好むそうですから、建材が自動的に酸性を和らげてくれるというわけです。ちなみに、黒メダカは見えづらいので、オレンジ色のメダカがオススメです。

By way of explanation, we considered using chemicals to prevent the mosquito larvae, but this seemed inadvisable if we intended to sprinkle this water on the plants. So we took advantage of the fact that medaka and goldfish like to eat the larvae.

We heard that if you line the bottom of the rain barrel with Oiso sand, bacteria that breed in the gaps between the grains will break down the waste excreted by the medaka. Water hyacinths or other aquatic plants thrive on this nutrient, providing a leafy cover and a comfortable environment for small fish like the medaka. So we decided to suppress the growth of mosquito larvae by creating an ecosystem in this manner. We were also concerned about the pH of the rainwater, which sometimes exhibited acidity below pH5. However, we found that this would reverse to a slightly alkaline value of pH8 in two weeks or less (see the photos on the right-hand page), possibly because of the materials used for the containers: concrete for the barrels, and hibachi braziers for the water pots on the second floor. These materials appear to automatically reduce the acidity of the rainwater—a good thing for medaka, which are partial to slightly alkaline water. By the way, I recommend orange medaka over black medaka, which are harder to see.

★54
もちろん前提として、外皮性能を高いレベルで確保しています。Ua値0.50、C値実測0.27。断熱・気密のほかに形態的な観点でいえば、直達日射制御の検討に時間を割きました。軒の深さ・高さ、ルーバーの密度はこの検討から導き出されています。

Needless to say, this is predicated on ensuring a high level of exterior surface performance, for which we obtained a UA value (overall heat transfer) of 0.50 and a C value (corresponding gap area) measured at 0.27. In addition to thermal insulation and airtightness, we took time to study structural means of controlling direct solar radiation, based on which we derived the depth and height of the eaves and the density of the louvers.

上:2018年3月26日降雨時、pH6
下:同年3月29日降雨時、pH9
Top: Acidity at time of rainfall on March 26, 2018: pH6
Bottom: Acidity at time of rainfall on March 29, 2018: pH9

等時間日影図6月25日
1日を通して開口部からの直達日射がない
Sun shadow diagram: June 25 (same time period).
Apertures receive no direct sunlight at any time of day.

等時間日影図8月25日
1日を通して開口部からの直達日射がない
Sun shadow diagram: August 25 (same time period).
Apertures receive no direct sunlight at any time of day.

等時間日影図12月25日
開口部からの直達日射がふんだんにある
Sun shadow diagram: December 25 (same time period).
Apertures receive ample direct sunlight.

Added to this effect is the pleasure of cultivating the louvers themselves. The stabilized soil is laterally perforated with holes the same size as pot seedlings, so one can easily install seedlings of any kind purchased from a home improvement store. Initially we planted only perennial herbs, so no transplanting was involved, but whenever we grow plants that flower or fruit, passersby call out to us. Some scold us for hanging the plants in this gravity-defying manner, while others ask if they can have some herbs to take home with them.

At first I worried about mosquito larvae in the rain barrels. I conducted an experiment by putting medaka (Japanese rice fish) in some of the barrels and not in others. However, I found that if the barrel holds about 60 liters, the rain naturally refills it often enough that virtually no larvae appear.

The medaka, on the other hand, proliferated so much that they became an attraction for neighborhood schoolkids. ★53

As a result of introducing an ecological cycle by using rainwater to create a cool spot, the exterior appearance of these workplaces came to differ considerably from those of the Apartments with a Small Restaurant. I used waist-high windows instead of full-height windows, adding small ventilation windows here and there. This makes it possible to place a desk next to the window and create a scenic space there.

The biggest difference is in the entrance, which uses a sliding door instead of a hinged door, thus making it easier to adjust the amount of breeze to let in via the green louvers. Sliding doors also allow one to let air in even when it's raining, thanks to the eaves. ★54

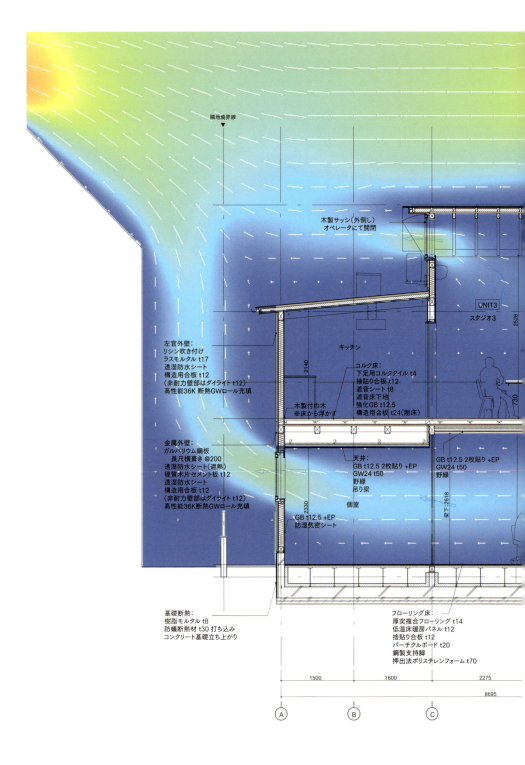

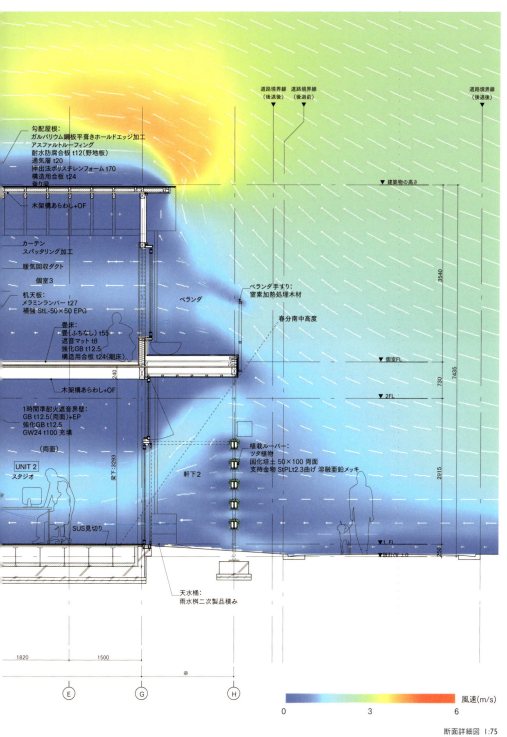

断面詳細図 1:75
Section detail 1:75

《五本木の集合住宅》は、地球規模の水の循環から見ればほんの一瞬だけ水を滞留させ、お裾分けをもらっている格好です。一般に、建築は雨に対して閉じています。雨漏りがあってはいけません。雨はなによりもまず避けるべきもの。一刻も早く流れ去るようにすべきです。しかし、この集合住宅では一人ひとりの天水桶に雨を一時的に貯めることで、温熱環境上の効用に繋げました。それも楽しみを伴うかたちで、です。

　この建築はそのための形態を持っています。仕組みが見えることが重要です。屋根や軒や植栽ルーバーといった建築のさまざまなエレメントに工夫を凝らし、それらを組み合わせました。地球規模の水の循環からお裾分けをもらって、中間領域としてのスタジオを開いています。人的な交流のために「開く」ことと、身体的に心地よいから「開く」ことを重ね合わせています。〈小さな経済〉という「Socialな循環」の場を、「Ecologicalな循環」のなかに位置づけようとした結果です。「2つの循環を重ねる」とは、こういうことを指しています★55。

★55
用途を複合させるとき、音の問題は軽視できません。特に床面の振動が伝わりやすい上下階間の遮音はとても重要です。《食堂付きアパート》はスパンを小さくしたうえでコンクリートスラブを敷設したために問題はありませんでしたが、《五本木の集合住宅》は木造なので慎重に設計しました。2階の床下地を軟質のゴム柱脚のものとしたり、下階の1階天井を天井用の梁から吊ったりすることで遮音性を確保し、集合住宅として良好な音環境を実現しています。詳しくは、仲俊治＋鈴木俊男「在来軸組工法を用いた2階建て木造建築スタジオの床衝撃実測結果」（日本建築学会大会学術講演梗概集、2018）を参照。

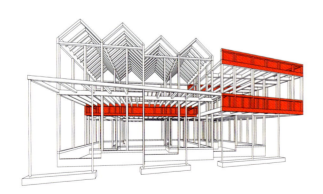

用途複合によって生じる複数の床梁を繋げて合成梁とし（赤色部分）、キャンチレバーや比較的長いスパンを実現している

To accommodate the multi-use format, we used cantilevers or relatively long spans for composite beams (shown in red) connecting multiple floor beams.

In the context of water cycles on a global scale, the Gohongi Housing retains and portions out just a tiny bit of water. Buildings are generally sealed off from the rain; leakage is impermissible. Rain is something to be kept out at all costs, to be diverted as rapidly as possible. Yet setting up rain barrels to temporarily store rainwater for each unit in this multi-unit house has had a beneficial effect on the thermal environment—and in a pleasure-giving format in the bargain.

The design of the building gives form to this function. It is important that the mechanism itself be visible. For this project I devised and combined several architectural elements—roof, eaves, green louvers—to form a system that enables us to retain and distribute a tiny portion of the global water cycle, and to open up the studios that serve as intermediate areas. They are "open" both to human interaction, and to comfortable physical contact with the outdoor environment. By thus locating places for the social cycle of small economies within an ecological cycle, we can achieve what I call the overlaying of the two cycles. ★55

★55
In multi-use housing, we cannot overlook the problem of noise. It is particularly difficult to provide soundproofing between upper and lower stories, since vibrations are so readily transmitted through the floor. In the Apartments with a Small Restaurant this was not a problem because the small spans allowed us to put down concrete slabs. The Gohongi Housing, however, is made of wood, so we proceeded with the design very cautiously. We used soft rubber column bases for the second-story subfloor and suspended the first-story ceiling from hanging beams, thus implementing soundproofing measures on both sides of the second-story floor. The result is an optimum acoustic environment for an apartment house. For further details, see Toshiharu Naka and Toshio Suzuki, "Results of Floor Impact Measurements in a Two-Story Wooden Studio Utilizing Conventional Post and Beam Construction" (*Summaries of Technical Papers of Annual Meeting, Architectural Institute of Japan, 2018*).

プロジェクト・コラム❸《西天満の集合住宅》(仮称)
Nishitemma Project (tentative name)

　大阪市の中心地に、5階建ての集合住宅を設計しています。ここでも2つの循環を重ね合わせようと考えています。敷地形状が細長いこともあって、中心に上下動線を設け、各住宅を向かい合わせて配置しています。向かい合い方に動きを持たせたいために、半階ずつずれたスキップフロア形式にしています。各住宅はそのなかで仕事もできるようにスタジオアクセスの構成を採っています。下階にはオーナー親族が営む飲食店を設け、住宅の一部もオーナーが使用することから、交流の核が明確な集合住宅になります。

　向かい合わせになった階段の踊り場を広く確保し、スタジオから続く、交換・交流のきっかけの場とします。大阪市内はたいへん暑く、また風の少ない時間帯があるので、《五本木の集合住宅》のように、雨と涼風を立体的につくりだそうと、検討を続けています。

I am designing a five-story apartment house in central Osaka. Here, too, I intend to overlay the two cycles. The site is long and narrow, so I have inserted a vertical line of flow through the center, across which apartment units face one another. To give movement to this oppositional relationship I have arranged it in a split-level format so that facing units are vertically staggered a half-story apart. Each unit has a studio-access layout so that work can be done on the premises. The ground floor contains a restaurant run by the family of the owner, who will also use part of the residential section. Therefore the entire complex will have a built-in core of sustainable interaction.

　The staircase landings across which the units face each other are extra wide so as to function as places of exchange and interaction by extension from the studios. Because downtown Osaka can get very hot, and there are times of day when there is little wind, I am studying ways to create three-dimensional access to rain and cooling breezes.

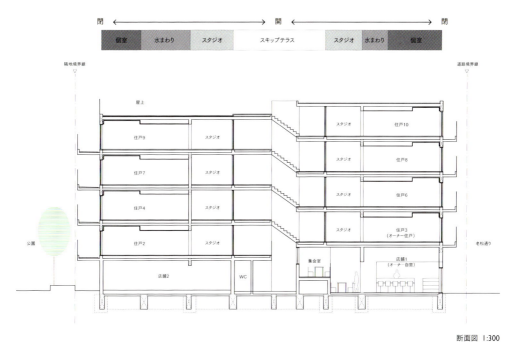

断面図 1:300
Section 1:300

4 Positioning Architecture within Two Cycles

4–2　動的なプログラム論——閾論のアップデート
Dynamic Program Theory: A Threshold Theory Update

　プログラム論とは、用途に応じた諸室とその配列についての議論を指します。《食堂付きアパート》や《五本木の集合住宅》で述べたスタジオアクセスの考え方はそれにあたります。

　これらの集合住宅は、住宅という用途に仕事場や食堂といった異なる用途を複合させたものです。ごちゃまぜ、とか、多用途、というだけではデザイン論にはなりません。異なる用途の境界面に着目し、それを空間化する。配列とともに空間のあり方に一定の論理を与える。それがプログラム論です。たとえば、建築家・山本理顕氏の「閾論（しきいろん）」はそのひとつですが、もともと、プログラム論は建築が社会的に機能するための議論から出発しているので、人間の関係性に主眼を置いてきました。本書でいえば、「Socialな循環」にあたります。

　下の図は、閾論を示すダイアグラムです。俗に「ひょうたんダイアグラム」と呼ばれるこの図は、社会における住宅の位置づけや内部空間の配列を示しています。山本氏は、「閾」を次のように定義しています。

　「『閾』とは2つの異なる領域の間にあって、その相互の関係を結びつけ、あるいは切り離すための空間である。都市という公的領域と家族という私的領域の中間にあって、その2つの領域を相互に結びつけ、あるいは切り離すための建築的な装置が『閾』である」★56。

　この図で強調されていることはもう一点あり、それは「閾」が住宅の中にあって、それでもなお公的領域に属する空間であるということです。山本氏はこの閾論によって、住宅の内部をすべて私的領域と思い込むことを批判し、さまざまな住宅や集合住宅をつくってきました。僕が関わった「地域社会圏」の研究は閾を持つ集合住宅モデルの研究ですし、山本氏のこの閾論から僕は多くの影響を受け、《食堂付きアパート》や《五本木の集合住宅》をつくることになりました。

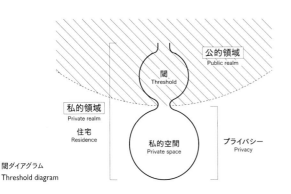

閾ダイアグラム
Threshold diagram

★56
山本理顕『権力の空間／空間の権力——個人と国家の〈あいだ〉を設計せよ』（講談社, 2015）24-25頁
Riken Yamamoto, *The Space of Power and the Power of Space: Designing Between Personal and State Spaces*, Kodansha, 2015, pp. 24-25.

Program theory refers to the study of architectural spaces and their arrangement according to purpose. The studio-access approach I discussed in regard to the Apartments with a Small Restaurant and the Gohongi Housing is an example of a program theory.

These multi-unit buildings combine residential with other types of use, specifically workplaces and a restaurant. Simply calling such arrangements multi-use, or a hodgepodge, is not sufficient for the purposes of design theory. One must study the interfaces between different uses and give them spatial form, imposing a consistent logic upon the format of these spaces along with their arrangements. This is what we mean by program theory. One example is the *shikii* (threshold) theory of the architect Riken Yamamoto. Program theory originated from debates over the function of architecture in society and therefore has focused primarily on human relations. In terms of my discussion in this book, it pertains to the social cycle.

On the left-hand page is a diagram illustrating threshold theory. It uses a gourd-shaped pattern to indicate the position of a residence in society and the layout of its interior spaces. Yamamoto defines "threshold" as follows:

"A threshold is a space between two different areas that serves to either connect or separate them. When placed between the public realm of the city and the private realm of the family, the threshold is an architectural device for bringing the two realms together or keeping them apart."★56

This diagram emphasizes another aspect as well: the threshold is located inside the residence, yet at the same time it is a space that belongs to the public realm. Through this threshold theory, Yamamoto critiqued the assumption that the entire interior of a residence is a private space, and he designed many types of house and apartment housing accordingly. The research undertaken by the Local Community Area Study Group in which I participated was a study of collective housing models with thresholds. Yamamoto's threshold theory had a great impact on me and served as an inspiration for my design of such projects as the Apartments with a Small Restaurant and the Gohongi Housing.

前節では「Socialな循環」と「Ecologicalな循環」という2つの循環を重ねて、日常的な交換の場をつくることを述べました。たとえばその交換の場は、「住宅の中の外向きの場所」としての仕事場です。《食堂付きアパート》や《五本木の集合住宅》におけるスタジオがそれにあたります。どちらの住宅もスタジオアクセスという形式を採っていて、それは、街路や共用廊下側にスタジオを配置し、その奥に私的空間が配置されるというものです。
　「Ecologicalな循環」への着目は、内外の境界面のあり方を扱うことに繋がります。
　すでに見てきたように、《上総喜望の郷おむかいさん》では、太陽熱を利用するための小さな屋根の形に一定の特徴が生まれました。構造的な観点から、隣接する傘ユニットの列柱の向きが相互に直交するという平面的な規則性が表れ、熱利用の観点から、南側の屋根は低く、北側の屋根は高くなるという断面的な規則性が表れました。
　《五本木の集合住宅》は、雨を小分けに集めるという目的から、小さく反復する固有の屋根――ギザギザ屋根の形が導き出されています。その雨を使ってクールスポットをつくりだそうとすることがルーバーや窓のデザインへと繋がり、厚みを持った表層を獲得しています。
　《白馬の山荘》の屋根形状や衣替えの工夫も、《深沢の住宅》の吹き抜けテラスを覆うグリーンルーバーも、内外の境界面が特徴的なデザインになっています。
　このように、「Socialな循環」に「Ecologicalな循環」を重ねるということは、従来のプログラム論から出発して、建築のシルエットや表層のあり方に固有の形態を見出すことに繋がります。これがとても面白い。結果として、どのような見え方＝アピアランス、になるのかという問題に接続されます。

プログラム・配列　→　プログラム・配列　＋　表層・アピアランス

　2つの循環を重ねることは、従来的なプログラム論をアップデートする作業のように考えています。
　「形態は機能に従う」とルイス・サリヴァン[57]は述べました。機能主義に基づく近代建築は内部の機能性を優先し、外形や表層はその結果であるとしました。機能の配列を示すダイアグラムは通常、太い枠線で縁取られています。従来的なプログラム論をアップデートするということは、この太い枠線が何でできていて、どのようにあればよいのかを問うことでもあります。
　太い枠線がもっと有機的な境界線になり、交換や交流を生むものになるという意味で、それは動的なプログラム論であるといえそうです。

In the previous section I discussed the creation of places for day-to-day exchange by overlaying two cycles, the social and the ecological. A workspace functioning as an "outward-oriented place" inside a residence is one such place of exchange, as exemplified by the studios in the Apartments with a Small Restaurant and the Gohongi Housing. In both buildings I applied the studio-access format in which the studio faces the street or common passageway and the private area is in the back.

How one incorporates an ecological cycle affects the character of the interior-exterior interface.

As I mentioned earlier, certain unique characteristics emerged from the small-roof format I designed to utilize solar heat for the Omukai-san facility. Structurally, the placement of the column rows of adjacent umbrella units at right angles to one another created a planar regularity in the layout, while the arrays of roof heights from low to high in the south-to-north direction for purposes of heat utilization created a cross-sectional regularity.

With the Gohongi Housing, the objective of subdividing collected rainfall led to an iterative design of small roofs in a zigzag configuration. Likewise the use of rainwater to form cool spots determined the design of the louvers and windows, producing a façade of substantial thickness.

The roof and the "wardrobe-changing" roofed plaza of the Villa in Hakuba, and the green louvers covering the atrium terrace of the House in Fukasawa, are also examples of how distinctive designs emerged for interior-exterior interfaces.

The overlaying of social and ecological cycles thus leads to the discovery of unique forms for building façades and silhouettes that depart from conventional program theory. It's an intriguing phenomenon, one linked to the question of what sort of appearance a building should have.

Program/Arrangement → Program/Arrangement + Surface/Appearance

I think of the overlaying of these two cycles as a process of updating program theory.

Louis Sullivan declared that "form follows function."[57] Functionalist modern architecture has prioritized the functionality of interiors and treated surfaces and external appearances as an outcome of that priority. Diagrams illustrating functional layouts generally frame them with thick borders. Updating conventional program theory entails questioning what those thick borders are actually made of, and how they should be designed. A dynamic program theory should be one that turns these thick borders into more organic interfaces that will foster exchanges and interactions.

[57]
ルイス・サリヴァン (1856-1924) はシカゴ派の建築家。シカゴ大火 (1871) 以後高層建築が席巻するなか、デザインを模索した建築家のひとりです。古典様式と決別し、鉄骨造の採用によって構造的な制約から逃れ、機能をデザインの軸に据えたとされます。
Louis Sullivan (1856-1924) was an architect of the Chicago School, known for his experiments with design as high-rise architecture surged to prominence in the aftermath of the Great Chicago Fire of 1871. As the use of steel-frame construction freed architects from classical styles and structural constraints, function became the pivotal issue of architectural design.

　《白馬の山荘》をつくったときに、施工を担当した地元の工務店の池田さんから、これは現代版の鞘だ、と評されたことがあります。鞘というのは、北信地域の蔵に用いられる伝統的な構法です。軒先を柱と貫からなる格子状のフレームで支えることで豪雪に耐える構法のことです。そしてその格子と蔵のあいだの軒下空間は、雪が積もらない貴重な外部として、藁を干したり、大根などの野菜を干すなどといったことに使われてきました。

　《白馬の山荘》では、伝統的な格子の代わりに、基礎に埋め込まれたハシゴ状の鉄骨の構造体があります。ハシゴ状になっているのは水平方向の荷重（風や地震）に対抗するためで、その役割は、伝統的な鞘構法と同じです。そして軒先にビニールカーテンを吊したり、それを蚊帳ネットに取り替えたりする際には、このハシゴを上って作業をします。大きな透明屋根に覆われた空間を活性化するために、この構造体が役立てられています。そのことを評して、池田さんは現代版の鞘だといったわけです。

When we were building the Villa in Hakuba, Mr. Ikeda, the local contractor in charge of construction, said it looked like a modern version of *saya*. The *saya* is a traditional construction method used for storehouses in northern Nagano Prefecture, in which a lattice-like frame of pillars and crosspieces supports the eaves to keep them from collapsing under heavy snows. The space under the eaves between this lattice and the storehouse wall is also sheltered from the snow and therefore serves as a valuable outdoor space for drying straw, root vegetables and the like.

Instead of a traditional lattice, the Villa in Hakuba has ladder-shaped steel frames embedded in the foundation. The ladder configuration is for bearing horizontal loads (wind, earthquakes) and in that sense functions like the traditional *saya*. The ladders are also for climbing in order to hang the vinyl curtain or mosquito netting from the eaves. This structure thus enhances the use of the space covered by the large transparent roof. That is the sense in which Mr. Ikeda praised it as "a modern version of *saya*."

What is interesting about comparing the two structures is that, while a *saya* frame is made of wood and that of the Villa in Hakuba is steel, they are identical in having a criss-cross configuration beneath the outer edge of the eaves. In designing eaves with a depth suited to heavy snows and ground-level access, I happened to arrive at the same structure used for traditional storehouses in Japan's snow country. This experience gave me a sense of the potential to be found in landscapes that transcend time.

Though similarly deep, the space under the Gohongi Housing eaves was designed to draw in the breeze. The deep eaves of houses in the Asian monsoon belt are emblematic of a history of creating architecture amid grand cycles of rain and wind. They are a feature born of the heat- and humidity-driven need to open windows and admit the breeze even on rainy days. The space beneath the eaves has become a place for daily human interaction and for work, resulting in townscapes of long rows of contiguous roofs and eaves.

I have a hunch that positioning architecture within both the social and ecological cycles will give birth to architecture, and communities composed of it, that support a day-to-day lifestyle conducive to self-reflection and harmonious relations with other people and the outside world.

Locating architecture within these two cycles will, I am convinced, transform communities on a scale beyond the appearance of individual structures.

ここで面白いのは、鞘のフレームをつくる材料は木から鉄へと更新されているものの、軒先に縦横に組まれているという点は同じであることです。大雪に耐え、地続きの出入りを叶える軒深さを獲得しようとして、同じ形式に辿り着いているわけです。ここに僕は、時代を超えた風景の可能性を感じます。

　深い軒は同じでも、《五本木の集合住宅》の軒下空間は風を取り入れるためのものです。

　アジアモンスーン地帯における軒深い建築には、雨と風の大きな循環のなかに建築を位置づけようとしてきた歴史を見ることができます。暑さや湿気ゆえに雨の日も窓を開けて風を取り入れたいからこその形式です。そして軒の下は人々の日常的な交流の舞台となり、生業の舞台となってきました。屋根が連なり、軒が続く、そんな都市の風景をつくりだしてきました。

　建築を2つの循環のなかに位置づけることの先には、自己を内省し、他者や外部に親和的な、そんな日常生活を支える建築とそれによってつくられる風景が現れる、といった予感があります。

　2つの循環のなかに建築を位置づけることは、個々の建築のアピアランスを超えて、風景の獲得まで辿り着けるのではないか、という期待を持たずにはいられません。

略歴

仲俊治
Toshiharu Naka

1976	京都府生まれ
1999	東京大学工学部建築学科卒業
2001	東京大学大学院工学系研究科建築学専攻修了
2001–08	山本理顕設計工場
2009	建築設計モノブモン設立（2012 株式会社仲建築設計スタジオに改組）
2009–11	横浜国立大学大学院 Y-GSA 設計助手
2011–14	東京都市大学非常勤講師
2013–19	横浜国立大学非常勤講師
2014–18	明治大学非常勤講師
2015–16	東京大学非常勤講師
2016–19	関東学院大学非常勤講師
2017–19	首都大学東京非常勤講師
2017–	法政大学大学院、東京理科大学大学院非常勤講師
2017–	グッドデザイン賞審査員
2018–	法政大学江戸東京研究センター客員研究員

主な書籍（共著、寄稿）

山本理顕ほか『地域社会圏主義 増補改訂版』（LIXIL出版、2013）
門脇耕三ほか『シェアの思想――または愛と制度と空間の関係』（LIXIL出版、2015）
山本理顕＋仲俊治『脱住宅――「小さな経済圏」を設計する』（平凡社、2018）

受賞歴

2009	横浜国立大学橋のコンセプト・デザインコンペ最優秀賞 横浜国立大学
2010	第18回リフォームデザインコンテスト2010新人賞《《茘の家》）日本増改築産業協会
2012	第44回中部建築賞金賞《《白馬の山荘》）中部建築賞協議会
2013	第1回LIXILデザインコンテスト2012銅賞《《白馬の山荘》）LIXIL
	第11回長野県建築文化賞優秀賞《《白馬の山荘》）長野県建築士会
2014	グッドデザイン2014金賞《《食堂付きアパート》）日本デザイン振興会
2015	第16回JIA環境建築賞優秀賞《《白馬の山荘》）日本建築家協会
	第31回吉岡賞《《食堂付きアパート》》新建築社
	2015年度JIA優秀建築選《《食堂付きアパート》）日本建築家協会
	住まいの環境デザイン・アワード2015優秀賞《《食堂付きアパート》）東京ガス
2016	2016年度JIA優秀建築選《《上総喜望の郷おむかいさん》）日本建築家協会
	第15回ヴェネチア・ビエンナーレ国際建築展審査員特別表彰
	（受賞対象は日本館。仲建築設計スタジオは出展作家のひとり）ビエンナーレ財団
	日本建築学会新人賞《《食堂付きアパート》）日本建築学会
	作品選集2016《《食堂付きアパート》）日本建築学会
2017	第23回千葉県建築文化賞優秀賞《《上総喜望の郷おむかいさん》）千葉県
	住まいの環境デザイン・アワード2017入賞《《上総喜望の郷おむかいさん》）東京ガス
2018	2018年度JIA優秀建築選《《五本木の集合住宅》）日本建築家協会
2019	住まいの環境デザイン・アワード2019グランプリ《《五本木の集合住宅》）東京ガス
	作品選集2019《《上総喜望の郷おむかいさん》）日本建築学会

Profile

1976	Born in Kyoto, Japan
1999	BA, Faculty of Engineering, University of Tokyo
2001	MA, Graduate School of Engineering, University of Tokyo
2001–08	Riken Yamamoto & Fieldshop
2009	Established Naka Architects' Studio
2009–11	Y-GSA design assistant
2011–14	Lecturer at Tokyo City University
2013–19	Lecturer at Yokohama National University
2014–18	Lecturer at Meiji University
2015–16	Lecturer at University of Tokyo
2016–19	Lecturer at Kanto Gakuin University
2017–	Lecturer at Hosei University, Tokyo University of Science, Tokyo Metropolitan University
2017–	Juror, Good Design Award
2018–	Guest Associate Researcher, Hosei University Research Center for Edo-Tokyo Studies

Publications (co-authored, contribution)

Riken Yamamoto et al., *Local Community Area Principles, revised and expanded edition* (LIXIL Publishing, 2013)
Kozo Kadowaki et al., *The Share Concept, or The Relationship between Love, Systems, and Spaces* (LIXIL Publishing, 2015)
Riken Yamamoto and Toshiharu Naka, *Beyond Residences: Designing "Small Economies"* (Heibonsha, 2018)

Awards

2009	First Prize, Competition for "Y.N.U. Bridge and Landscape Design" (Yokohama National Univ.)
2010	18th JERCO Renovation Award for "Sai"
2012	44th Chubu Architectural Award for "Villa in Hakuba"
2013	1st LIXIL Design Contest Bronze Prize for "Villa in Hakuba"
	11th Nagano Prefecture Architectural Award for "Villa in Hakuba"
2014	Good Design Gold Award for "Apartments with a Small Restaurant"
2015	16th JIA Sustainable Architecture Award Second Prize for "Villa in Hakuba"
	31st Yoshioka Award for "Apartments with a Small Restaurant"
	JIA Selected 100 Works for "Apartments with a Small Restaurant"
	Tokyo Gas Living Environmental Design Award for "Apartments with a Small Restaurant"
2016	JIA Selected 100 Works for "Houses for People with ID"
	Special Mention for the Japan Pavilion of the 15th Venice Biennale
	AIJ Young Architects Award for "Apartments with a Small Restaurant"
	AIJ Selected Architectural Designs for "Apartments with a Small Restaurant"
2017	23rd Architecture Award of Chiba Prefecture for "Houses for People with ID"
	Tokyo Gas Living Environmental Design Award for "Houses for People with ID"
2018	JIA Selected 100 Works for "Gohongi Housing"
2019	Tokyo Gas Living Environmental Design Award for "Gohongi Housing"
	AIJ Selected Architectural Designs for "Houses for People with ID"

プロジェクト

	作品名	用途	担当	延べ面積	所在地/計画地	備考
2010	載の家	専用住宅 (改修)	仲俊治、宇野悠里	223.03㎡	東京都	
2010	Y-GSA Power Plant Studio	大学施設 (改修)	仲俊治、宇野悠里	590.4㎡	神奈川県	※共同設計 Y-GSAスタジオコミッティ、末光弘和
2010	八ヶ岳の山荘	週末住宅	仲俊治、宇野悠里	90.38㎡	山梨県	
2010	C Project	ホテルほか	仲俊治、宇野悠里	17,780㎡	北海道	※共同設計 スターパイロッツ
2011	白馬の山荘	週末住宅	仲俊治、宇野悠里、佐藤謙太郎、福間浩之	84.16㎡	長野県	
2011	地域社会圏 鶴見モデル	共同住宅ほか	仲俊治、宇野悠里	42,619㎡	神奈川県	※共同研究 山本理顕、末光弘和、松行輝昌
2012	413号室改修	共同住宅の住戸 (改修)	仲俊治、宇野悠里、佐藤謙太郎	38.00㎡	東京都	
2014	食堂付きアパート	共同住宅、食堂、シェアオフィス	仲俊治、宇野悠里、佐藤謙太郎、上月亮太	261.13㎡	東京都	
2014	W chair	家具	仲俊治、宇野悠里、上月亮太			
2014	深沢の住宅	専用住宅	仲俊治、宇野悠里、佐藤謙太郎	116.76㎡	東京都	
2014	喜望の郷改修	福祉施設 (改修)	仲俊治、宇野悠里、佐藤謙太郎、上月亮太	521.91㎡	千葉県	
2015	上総喜望の郷 おむかいさん	福祉施設	仲俊治、宇野悠里、後藤昌子、佐藤謙太郎、上月亮太、久保祐里子	1,108.51㎡	千葉県	※設計協力 川島真由美建築デザイン
2015	小さな経済の住宅	兼用住宅 (モデルルーム)	仲俊治、宇野悠里	33.29㎡		
2015	音楽家の スタジオ付き住宅	兼用住宅 (改修)	仲俊治、宇野悠里	85.21㎡	東京都	
2016	国立科学博物館 ルーフトップテラス	博物館 (改修)	仲俊治、宇野悠里	721.70㎡	東京都	※共同設計 廣部剛司建築研究所
2016	小商いの実験室	コミュニティカフェ (改修)	仲俊治、宇野悠里、久保祐里子	81.59㎡	東京都	
2017	203号室改修	共同住宅の住戸 (改修)	仲俊治、宇野悠里	69.48㎡	東京都	
2017	ゆうゆうの郷改修	福祉施設 (改修)	仲俊治、宇野悠里	186.25㎡	千葉県	
2017	写真家の スタジオ付き住宅	兼用住宅	仲俊治、宇野悠里、後藤昌子	155.92㎡	群馬県	
2017	五本木の集合住宅	兼用住宅による長屋	仲俊治、宇野悠里、久保祐里子	219.46㎡	東京都	
2018	緑町の集合住宅	兼用住宅による長屋	仲俊治、宇野悠里、後藤昌子、諸星佑香	162.51㎡	東京都	
2018	白金の集合住宅	共同住宅	仲俊治、宇野悠里、後藤昌子	270.09㎡	東京都	
2019	高架下の小商い空間 MA-TO	シェアキッチン、店舗 ほか	仲俊治、宇野悠里、宮下巧大、諸星佑香	175.72㎡	東京都	
2019 (予定)	(仮称) 我孫子のグループホーム	福祉施設	仲俊治、宇野悠里、宮下巧大	250.62㎡	千葉県	
2020 (予定)	(仮称) 西天満プロジェクト	共同住宅、食堂、店舗	仲俊治、宇野悠里、宮下巧大	964.84㎡	大阪府	

Projects

Year	Name	Program	Project Team	Total Floor Area	Location	Co-designer etc.
2010	Sai	Residence (renovation)	Toshiharu Naka, Yuri Uno	223.03㎡	Tokyo	
2010	Y-GSA Power Plant Studio	University facility (renovation)	Toshiharu Naka, Yuri Uno	590.4㎡	Kanagawa	Joint design: Y-GSA Studio Committee, Hirokazu Suemitsu
2010	Villa in Yatsugatake	Weekend residence	Toshiharu Naka, Yuri Uno	90.38㎡	Yamanashi	
2010	C Project	Hotel etc.	Toshiharu Naka, Yuri Uno	17,780㎡	Hokkaido	Joint design: STARPILOTS
2011	Villa in Hakuba	Weekend residence	Toshiharu Naka, Yuri Uno, Kentaro Sato, Hiroyuki Fukuma	84.16㎡	Nagano	
2011	Local Community Area Tsurumi Model	Apartment housing, etc.	Toshiharu Naka, Yuri Uno	42,619㎡	Kanagawa	Joint research: Riken Yamamoto, Hirokazu Suemitsu, Terumasa Matsuyuki
2012	#413 Renovation	Apartment unit (renovation)	Toshiharu Naka, Yuri Uno, Kentaro Sato	38.00㎡	Tokyo	
2014	Apartments with a Small Restaurant	Apartments, restaurant, shared office	Toshiharu Naka, Yuri Uno, Kentaro Sato, Ryota Kozuki	261.13㎡	Tokyo	
2014	W chair	Furniture	Toshiharu Naka, Yuri Uno, Ryota Kozuki			
2014	House in Fukasawa	Residence (renovation)	Toshiharu Naka, Yuri Uno, Kentaro Sato	116.76㎡	Tokyo	
2014	Kibou no Sato (Renovation)	Care facility (renovation)	Toshiharu Naka, Yuri Uno, Kentaro Sato, Ryota Kozuki	521.91㎡	Chiba	
2015	Omukai-san	Care facility (renovation)	Toshiharu Naka, Yuri Uno, Shoko Goto, Kentaro Sato, Ryota Kozuki, Yuriko Kubo	1,108.51㎡	Chiba	Design cooperation: Kawashima Mayumi Architects Design
2015	'Small Economy' House	Mixed-use housing (model room)	Toshiharu Naka, Yuri Uno	33.29㎡		
2015	Musician's House with Studio (Renovation)	Mixed-use housing (renovation)	Toshiharu Naka, Yuri Uno	85.21㎡	Tokyo	
2016	Rooftop Renovation of N.M.N.S.	Museum (renovation)	Toshiharu Naka, Yuri Uno	721.70㎡	Tokyo	Joint design: Takeshi Hirobe Architects
2016	Small Business Laboratory	Community cafe (renovation)	Toshiharu Naka, Yuri Uno, Yuriko Kubo	81.59㎡	Tokyo	
2017	#203 Renovation	Apartment unit (renovation)	Toshiharu Naka, Yuri Uno	69.48㎡	Tokyo	
2017	Yuyu no Sato (Renovation)	Care facility (renovation)	Toshiharu Naka, Yuri Uno	186.25㎡	Chiba	
2017	Photographer's House with Studio	Mixed-use housing	Toshiharu Naka, Yuri Uno, Shoko Goto	155.92㎡	Gunma	
2017	Gohongi Housing	Mixed-use row house	Toshiharu Naka, Yuri Uno, Yuriko Kubo	219.46㎡	Tokyo	
2018	Midoricho Housing	Mixed-use row house	Toshiharu Naka, Yuri Uno, Shoko Goto, Yuka Morohoshi	162.51㎡	Tokyo	
2018	Shirogane Housing	Apartment house	Toshiharu Naka, Yuri Uno, Shoko Goto	270.09㎡	Tokyo	
2019	Small Economy under Railway	Shared kitchen, shops, etc.	Toshiharu Naka, Yuri Uno, Kohdai Miyashita, Yuka Morohoshi	175.72㎡	Tokyo	
2019 (planned)	Group Home in Abiko	Care facility (renovation)	Toshiharu Naka, Yuri Uno, Kohdai Miyashita	250.62㎡	Chiba	
2020 (planned)	Nishitemma Project	Apartments, restaurant, shops	Toshiharu Naka, Yuri Uno, Kohdai Miyashita	964.84㎡	Osaka	

クレジット

写真	鳥村鋼一／pp. 8-9、10-11、16-17、18-19、20-21、23、24-25、38（上下）、40、42-43、49（上中下）、70-71、74、76、80（右）、82、98-99、101、102、124-125、130（上下）、131、134（上下）、135、139、149、152	
	吉田誠／pp. 44（下）、88、90、91	
	西川公朗／pp. 86-87、96-97、117	
	新建築社写真部／pp. 81、155	
	HITOTOWA INC.／pp. 52-53	
	植原正太郎／p. 41	
	仲建築設計スタジオ／上記以外	

そのほか
- p. 26　かけはぎ業従業者数、ミシン出荷台数の変遷／総務省統計局経済センサス、経済産業省機械統計年報をもとに筆者作成
- p. 64　51C-N型／引用出典＝鈴木成文『51C白書──私の建築計画学戦後史』（住まいの図書館出版局、2006）169頁
- p. 66　葛西クリーンタウン清新北ハイツ4-9号棟／
引用出典＝森保洋之ほか『建築計画・設計シリーズ4 高層・超高層集合住宅』（市ヶ谷出版社、1993）108頁
- p. 67　スクエア玉川上水／引用出典＝日本建築学会編『第2版 コンパクト建築設計資料集成［住居］』（丸善出版、2006）137頁
- p. 115　人生のなかで他人に頼る時期／引用出典＝大月敏雄『住まいと町とコミュニティ』（王国社、2017）7頁
- p. 120　スパコンを使ったシミュレーション例（部分）／
引用出典＝国土交通省国土技術政策総合研究所「地区スケールの『風の道』のイメージの例」
（http://www.nilim.go.jp/lab/bcg/siryou/tnn/tnn0730pdf/ks073010.pdf）
- p. 148　閾ダイアグラム／山本理顕『権力の空間／空間の権力──個人と国家の〈あいだ〉を設計せよ』（講談社、2015）25頁をもとに、著者承諾を得て字句を改変

現代建築家コンセプト・シリーズ26
仲俊治｜2つの循環

発行日	2019年7月10日　第1刷発行
著者	仲俊治
発行者	佐竹葉子
発行所	LIXIL出版 〒104-0031 東京都中央区京橋3-6-18 TEL. 03-5250-6571　FAX. 03-5250-6549 http://www.livingculture.lixil/publish/
企画・編集	飯尾次郎（スペルプラーツ）
翻訳	アラン・グリースン
デザイン	浅田農（MATCH and Company Co., Ltd.）
制作協力	諸星佑香、宮下巧大、滝澤正啓、李熙徳（仲建築設計スタジオ）
印刷	株式会社加藤文明社

ISBN978-4-86480-042-6 C0352
© 2019 by Toshiharu Naka. Printed in Japan

乱丁・落丁本はLIXIL出版までお送りください。
送料負担にてお取り替えいたします。